S0-ALE-893

DOES THIS SOUND FAMILIAR?

- He won't wear his sweater because it's too itchy.
- When relatives visit, she retreats to her room.
- A wrong answer at school results in a flood of tears.
- It's too loud.
- It's too hot.
- Nothing tastes good.
- Everything is scary.

Impossible and inconsolable are terms usually associated with highly sensitive children. But these negative labels can be removed, as parents learn to identify the special needs of a child whose innate temperament is often in conflict with the world.

If you've been struggling to raise your sensitive child, help is on the way. *The Sensitive Child* will show you how to help your son or daughter cope with life and, ultimately, to be the best he or she can be.

Also by Janet Poland
The Magical Years series

GETTING TO KNOW YOUR ONE-YEAR-OLD
SURVIVING YOUR TWO-YEAR-OLD
MAKING FRIENDS WITH YOUR THREE-YEAR-OLD

St. Martin's Paperbacks titles are available at quantity discounts for sales promotions, premiums or fund raising. Special books or book excerpts can also be created to fit specific needs. For information write to special sales manager, St. Martin's Press, 175 Fifth Avenue, New York, N.Y. 10010.

You can get any St. Martin's Paperbacks title in print. For every book ordered, please send title and retail price, plus $1.50 for the first title and 50¢ for each title thereafter, to cover postage and handling. Send check or money order, or charge to your VISA, MASTERCARD, DISCOVER or AMERICAN EXPRESS card—no cash or CODs. New York residents add applicable sales tax. Mail to: Publishers Book and Audio Mailing Service, P.O. Box 120159, Staten Island, NY 10312–0004.

THE
SENSITIVE
CHILD

JANET POLAND

JUDI CRAIG, PH.D.,
Consulting Editor

A Skylight Press Book

St. Martin's Paperbacks

NOTE: If you purchased this book without a cover you should be aware that this book is stolen property. It was reported as "unsold and destroyed" to the publisher, and neither the author nor the publisher has received any payment for this "stripped book."

Published by arrangement with Skylight Press, 260 West 72nd Street, Suite 6C, New York, NY 10023.

THE CHALLENGING CHILD: THE SENSITIVE CHILD

Copyright © 1995 by Skylight Press.

Cover photograph by Peter Brandt.

All rights reserved. No part of this book may be used or reproduced in any manner whatsoever without written permission except in the case of brief quotations embodied in critical articles or reviews. For information address St. Martin's Press, 175 Fifth Avenue, New York, N.Y. 10010.

ISBN: 0-312-95931-1

Printed in the United States of America

St. Martin's Paperbacks edition/August 1996

10 9 8 7 6 5 4 3 2 1

Contents

CONTENTS

Foreword

The word *sensitive* conjures up different images, both positive and negative, to different people. Especially when you're talking about a child's personality or temperament.

What comes to mind might be a child who is unusually fussy and picky, whether it be over clothes that are too "scratchy," food that gags, weird smells, or noises from vacuum cleaners and hair dryers. It might be a child who doesn't like unpredictability, fast-paced activity, and too many people around (like at the mall). It might be a child who is unusually shy or solitary, or one who is painfully anxious about social contact. It might be a child who is unusually perceptive and intuitive. Or it might be a child who "wears her feelings on her sleeve" and is easily hurt.

In my own clinical practice, I can see the frustration, irritation, and anguish in parents' eyes as they discuss these "sensitive" behaviors. Typically, they worry that they have done something wrong, that they have fallen into the dreaded category of "bad parents." A critical part of therapy for these children and their families often revolves around *education*, helping parents understand that "sensitivity" is frequently a dimension of a child's temperament and/or neurological wiring. Sensitive behaviors can also originate or be exacerbated by environmental factors that are out of a parents' control, such as a negative traumatic experience involving an accident, hospitalization, the weather, timing of a parent's absence, teasing by peers, or other coincidental but unlucky occurrences. Such events can lay the groundwork for anxiety or for exaggerated responses to normal noises and events.

Successful treatment also involves *encouragement*, both to the parents and to the child, that sensitive behaviors can be managed, modified, and compensated for. As these children grow up, they become better able to handle their own sensitivities and even begin to see the positive side of their own uniqueness.

It also helps greatly for parents to have some genuine guidelines for dealing with the kinds of everyday problems they are likely to encounter with these children. In *The Sensitive Child*, Janet Poland does a terrific job of giving practical advice for parents who are dealing with all types of sensitive behaviors. Combining a nice blend of research on temperament with good parenting psychology, she liberally sprinkles examples of the behaviors the sensitive child presents on a daily basis, points out common parental pitfalls, and gives appropriate strategies to deal with them.

She also addresses the issue of temperamental "fit" between parent and child and how to cope with the advantages and disadvantages posed by the matches and mismatches. She guides the reader through what sensitivity feels like "from the inside" and discusses the special circumstances and situations that make it more problematic.

The book concludes with considerations about the kind of adult the sensitive child can become, paying due respect to the many advantages of such a temperament, and closes with common questions a reader might ask.

Poland has taken a complicated subject and made it understandable. Her insights and common sense strategies should greatly benefit any parent of a child who often is easily misunderstood due to his or her own unique temperamental nature. As a therapist, passing this book on to a distraught parent will make my job a whole lot easier!

Judi Craig, Ph.D.
Clinical Psychologist, Author and Speaker

THE
SENSITIVE
CHILD

Understanding Sensitivity: Recognizing and Interpreting Your Child's Temperament

When Andrew was born, he inherited his brother's bedroom, his crib, and his baby clothes.

But Andrew did not inherit Jeremy's outgoing, happy-go-lucky personality.

Jeremy had been a hearty, uncritical eater. When he grew sleepy, he'd fall asleep anywhere. He welcomed every new day, delighted in every new adventure, and smiled at every stranger.

Then came Andrew. From the first weeks of life, he was a light sleeper and a tentative eater. He was easily startled, and he screamed during his baths. For the first time, his parents noticed how close the nursery was to the stairs (the tread of footsteps had never seemed to bother Jeremy), and how the morning sun streamed in the window, wakening Andrew at dawn. As he grew older, Andrew spit out new foods, hated his new shoes, and ran away from visitors.

"Jeremy was totally different," recalls the boys'

mother. "He was cooperative and sunny, and we thought that's how babies were. We thought we'd got it all down pretty well. Then Andrew came along, and we had to learn everything over."

Now that Andrew is ready for kindergarten, his parents worry not only about how best to raise him in the here and now, but about what the future holds as well. Will someone so shy and tentative ever have friends? Will someone so sensitive ever be tough enough to make his way in the real world?

Raising any child these days is a challenge, but some children are more challenging than others. The Challenging Child series is about those children whose distinct temperament brings particular difficulties; both the sensitive child and the demanding child require a different approach toward discipline, social experiences, emotional support, and the building of self-esteem and confidence.

That's because—according to the most recent findings in psychology, neurology, and genetics—temperament is as much a part of a child's innate individuality as the color of his hair or the shape of his nose.

And these rich differences in human temperament reflect traits that have endured through the generations because they have survival value. Just as the aggressive, courageous early human was suited to hunting food and defending family, his cautious, wary cousin may have survived dangers because of that careful temperament.

Because temperament affects how we approach other people, how we respond to limits, how we handle our fears and worries, we need to take it into account when we discipline our children, comfort them, and introduce them to the world. And we need to talk to our children about temperament and teach them ways to make the most of their gifts.

This book is for the parents of children for whom one or more of the following traits apply. Sensitive children may be:

- Unusually fussy about the feel of clothing, the texture or aroma of food, the temperature of the room or the bath water.
- Unusually shy, slow to participate in social situations, or solitary by preference.
- Unusually anxious, fearful, or easily wounded in social situations.
- Unusually uncomfortable with change, transitions, and new experiences (whether those new experiences are positive or negative).
- Unusually stressed by fast-paced activity or noisy, unpredictable environments.
- Unusually intuitive, perceptive, discerning, or "tuned in" to feelings and motives of their own or those of others.

Please note the use of the term "unusually." *All* children are wary or shy at certain times, at certain ages, and in certain settings. But sensitive children are consistently *more so* than their peers.

And although sensitive children are not average, they are normal. The range of normal behavior is broad, and sensitive children are part of that broad spectrum. With a few exceptions, all the behaviors discussed in this book are normal and healthy. In fact, sensitive children have strengths and gifts that can enrich their own lives and contribute to the family, community, and world.

WHAT SENSITIVE CHILDREN HAVE IN COMMON

Not all sensitive children are alike. As we'll discuss later in this chapter, there are four general styles of sensitivity, each with its distinct way of feeling and behaving. But all sensitive children share these fundamental similarities:

1. Sensitive children are aware of, and often distressed by, stimuli and experiences that are less noticeable or upsetting to other children.
2. Sensitive children are, usually, sensitive from infancy and will probably remain so, to some degree, throughout life.
3. Sensitivity can bring problems and blessings, depending on how parents structure their children's lives and help them manage and perceive their own behavior.

Too often, advice about raising children assumes they all come from the same mold. Tantrums, toilet training, and nightmares all get one-size-fits-all recommendations. But, as any parent of more than one child can attest—and Andrew's parents would second—that's rarely realistic. One approach may work with the older child and fail completely with the second.

If your cautious, eager-to please older child forgets the rules, you can probably do very well with a gentle reminder: "Anna, remember: While we're at Grandma's house, we don't bring food into the living room."

If Anna's little sister, however, is a fearless, impulsive, combative bundle of energy, your gentle reminder may be woefully inadequate.

Whether you have one child or five, your understanding of the role of temperament will help you in your efforts to be a wise, understanding, and effective parent.

WHAT IS SENSITIVITY?

First, let's take a look at what sensitivity is—and is not.

The word itself has both positive and negative connotations. The phrase, "He's so sensitive!" can refer to a wonderfully thoughtful and enlightened husband, or it can refer to someone who is so irritable and testy he can't take the slightest criticism.

But this book is about sensitivity in a broader sense. It's about a range of behaviors that persist, to some degree, throughout life and probably combine biological origins with the imprint of experience. Sensitive people have heightened reactions, are capable of responding to fainter stimuli, and have more pronounced fear responses than others.

The term also conjures up the image of the idea of the artistic, creative, sensitive soul. But sensitive people as we define them are not automatically thoughtful, considerate, or fond of poetry, although they may have a greater potential to feel and show compassion and to respond to music and art.

And the sensitivity that this book focuses on goes deeper than the kind of normal shyness or wariness that just about every child exhibits from time to time. When a two-year-old is fussy about his food, prone to nightmares, and afraid of strangers, he's not necessarily being sensitive. He's acting his age. Just as an energetic toddler who never stops from dawn to dusk is not necessarily hyperactive, a two-year-old who is sometimes bashful and easily upset may not be sensitive in the true, temperamental sense.

While this book will help parents deal with the kind of everyday "sensitive moments" that nearly all children encounter, its broader scope is the child who is fundamentally sensitive.

Such a child has plenty of company. Shyness, for example, is just one of the categories of sensitivity this book addresses (and which are outlined below). Yet researchers estimate that about 20 percent of American babies are born with a tendency toward extreme discomfort in social situations, and many more—more than 40 percent—grow up to define themselves as shy whether they were born that way or not.

IDENTIFYING YOUR SENSITIVE CHILD'S STYLE

Much of the current body of knowledge about temperament and children is attributable to the work of Stella Chess and Alexander Thomas, two psychologists who conducted one of the first studies of temperament, the New York Longitudinal Study, beginning in 1956. They began with a group of infants and followed their development at regular intervals until most were adolescents (they are continuing to study the group into adulthood). What they concluded was that different temperaments are observable early in life, persist throughout childhood, and call for specific child-rearing techniques.

Chess and Thomas categorized their group of children into "easy," "slow-to-warm-up," and "difficult," depending on the distribution of nine temperamental traits:

- Activity level
- Rhythmicity (regularity of functions like eating, sleeping, elimination)
- Approach or withdrawal (initial response to new situations)
- Adaptability

- Sensory threshold
- Quality of mood (generally pleasant, or generally negative)
- Intensity of reaction
- Distractibility
- Persistence and attention span.

Certainly an "easy" child would be cheerful, not overly active, reasonably regular in habits, and not too fussy about food and clothing. "Difficult" children might include energetic, persistent, irregular, fussy children who "dig in" and resist direction.

"Slow-to-warm-up" refers to negative initial reaction and slow adaptability. Many sensitive children, as described in this book, have those qualities, along with low sensory threshold and a high persistence.

For the purpose of this book, we're looking at sensitivity in a broader sense, and breaking it down into four categories that reflect recent scientific insights into temperament. Each of the following styles of sensitivity represents a predisposition that is probably rooted in biology, and thus each style calls for a different parenting approach.

Low Sensory Threshold

Andrew, as you recall, has always been sensitive to visual and auditory stimulation. Light wakes him up, whether it's the morning sun or passing headlights when he's sleeping in the car. He fusses over his food and startles when a balloon pops at a birthday party. Andrew belongs to one group of sensitive children who have heightened reactivity to stimuli from the senses—it takes less of a stimulus to elicit a reaction.

Some children in this group react to very low levels of light and sound; other children pick up and react to faint odors, slight differences in temperature, and different consistencies in food. The child who wears water shoes in the pool because he says the rough bottom hurts his feet, or the child who refuses to drink the kind of orange juice that has pulp in it because it "feels funny" probably has a low sensory threshold.

Your child may have a low sensory threshold if he exhibits some of these behaviors:

- Dislikes being bathed or changed as an infant.
- Dislikes new clothes, complains about stiff fabric or scratchy tags, takes time breaking in new shoes.
- Complains that the water is too hot or too cold in the bathtub or swimming pool.
- Is put off by unfamiliar or unpleasant smells.
- Gags on new or disliked foods.

Social Sensitivity

The socially sensitive child has difficulty with either the uncertainty or the stress of interactions with other people, especially unfamiliar people, or people who may be in a position to judge or evaluate him.

Certainly shyness is included here. But not all social sensitivity is the same. In this book, we make a distinction between the shy child, who is anxious about social interaction, and the solitary child, who chooses to isolate himself. Both are sensitive, but in different ways. Consider these girls, one shy, one with a preference for solitude.

At nine, Natasha has never ordered a meal in a restaurant. She is perfectly able to behave herself and use the proper cutlery, but she refuses to speak to waiters and waitresses. When she has made her selection from the menu, she whispers her request to her mother, who orders for her.

When Andrea's mother went to her daughter's kindergarten Back-to-School Night, she was concerned when the teacher told her that Andrea had not made any friends and was always playing by herself at recess. Then she remembered that even at parties and playdates at home, Andrea often drifts off to play by herself. Yet if asked, Andrea will say that she is, indeed, having fun.

Social sensitivity includes the classical shyness and fearfulness in group situations. But it also includes a preference for small group activities and solitary pleasures. True shyness is characterized by distress in the social situation; solitary behavior is marked by a preference for one's own company.

In a nursery school setting, for example, one

child may hover at the edge of a group of children, watching them intently but unable or unwilling to approach. Another child may also be playing alone, but playing happily with a puzzle or blocks.

Whether shy or solitary, the socially sensitive child experiences stress in social situations. Withdrawing from interactions is a way of relaxing, decompressing, reducing the stress.

Your child may be socially sensitive if he exhibits some of these behaviors:

- Is very cautious or uneasy in group situations.
- Dislikes meeting new people; is comfortable with familiar friends only.
- Grows anxious in anticipation of new situations, like the first day of school, a party, or a performance.
- Seems to enjoy being alone.
- Keeps his feelings and thoughts to himself.

Because true shyness in the traditional sense, is such a major aspect of sensitivity, and because it causes parents so much concern, we've given this topic its own chapter (Chapter Seven).

Emotional Sensitivity

Josh is getting ready for school. His fifth grade class is planning a field trip to the county courthouse. Josh is full of anxious questions as he heads out the door.

"What if I get lost?"

"What if I have to go to the bathroom and we're still on the bus?"

"What if a prisoner gets loose from the jail?"

Emotionally sensitive children like Josh may or may not be shy. They may have many friends or few. What they have in common is that they are prone to anxieties and worries, often seemingly groundless.

Those worries come in different forms. Some, like Josh's, are about vague, formless disasters. Other children worry more about making mistakes in school, forgetting lines in the school play, or about displeasing or disappointing others.

Emotionally sensitive children seem to have invisible antennae that pick up emotional tension in others, real or imagined.

One emotionally sensitive seven-year-old ran into the kitchen, where his parents had been talking and the father had spoken sarcastically about an acquaintance. "Are you mad at Mommy, or are you just using a mad voice?" the child inquired.

Emotionally sensitive children may be particularly vulnerable to scary stories or movies full of fear, anger, and violence.

They often have difficulties in social situations because of their tendency to overreact to slights, whether real or perceived. Such children may not be shy, but they often have difficulty with the ups and downs of childhood friendships, and the teasing and put-downs that are everyday occurrences.

Your child may be emotionally sensitive if he exhibits some of these behaviors:

- Asks a lot of anxious "What-if?" questions.
- Gets upset at minor mistakes and failures.
- Is a perfectionist.
- Cries easily.
- Has difficulty with teasing, no matter how good-natured.
- Shows intensity in whatever he does.
- Is perceptive beyond his years about other people's feelings.
- Worries about hurting other people's feelings.
- May be almost too good or too compliant.

Sensitivity to Change

Lauren, age seven, hates birthday parties. Even at her own party, Lauren had a hard time getting through the present-opening process; as soon as she unwrapped a set of doll clothes, she wanted to concentrate on enjoying it, rather than putting it aside and moving on to the next gift.

At other children's parties, any particular activity—making party hats, playing a circle game, singing, chasing balloons around the room—would suit Lauren just fine, if only she could do that one thing at her own pace.

But it's the rapid pileup of events and energy that Lauren finds so difficult to take. Usually, long before it's time to go home, Lauren ends up either in tears or playing by herself in the next room.

Lauren is not shy, nor is she unsociable. She has several good friends and relates well to others. Her variety of sensitivity is such that she prefers novelty in small doses. She is not adaptable; she has difficulty switching gears.

Five-year-old Miguel's family ordered new furniture for the family room. When the delivery truck arrived, Miguel's sisters were thrilled. They watched the workers hoist up the old, well-worn couch, carry it out the door, and replace it with a beautiful new one. They admired the new couch and tested its comfort.

Miguel, however, was devastated. His home looked different. His cozy old couch was gone. Everything was changed, and Miguel stated plainly that he "hated the new couch." Within a few days, however, Miguel came around and accepted the new furniture.

Other children who are sensitive to change may have trouble at shopping malls, carnivals, amusement parks, crowds, or even the unavoidable bane of family existence, the supermarket. Any environment that hums with activity and excitement and noise can be difficult for the child with this style of sensitivity.

Your child may be sensitive to change if he exhibits some of the following behaviors:

- Prefers sedentary activities to active ones.
- Dislikes high-energy, high-speed entertainment or activities.

- Has difficulty changing from one activity to another.
- Dislikes being rushed or hurried.
- Prefers routine to unstructured activities.
- Dislikes new situations, even pleasant ones.

You can see that this book can actually cover some very different children. One child (like Josh) wears his heart on his sleeve, keeping up a constant chatter about his worries and anxieties and observations. His parents may occasionally wish he'd be more inhibited about his feelings and frets. Yet another child may be quiet, slow to offer comments about anything, and be reluctant to tell his parents what he is thinking or feeling.

Your sensitive child, of course, may exhibit only some of these characteristics. But whatever kind of sensitivity your child exhibits, one thing is likely to emerge from this description: Some traits appear positive, some traits appear to present challenges. That is one of the keys to understanding sensitivity, and temperament in general. Nearly every temperamental trait can be a strength, if it's recognized, identified in postitive terms, moderated when necessary, and accepted by the child as part of his unique human endowment.

In this book, we will discuss children who are still coming to terms with their temperament birthright. Generally, we're focusing on children who have left infancy behind but have not yet reached adolescence. During these years, children gradually develop their muscles, their intellectual skills, and their emotional strength and independence. You, as the parent of a sensitive child, will be the primary force (along with teachers and other influential adults) in guiding this development, day by day.

By the way, both boys and girls can be sensitive. In this book, we use masculine pronouns like "he" and "his" in odd-numbered chapters, and "she" and "hers" in even-numbered chapters. Whatever the gender of the pronoun, or of a child in a particular example, the suggestions and points usually apply to boys and girls.

The purpose of this book is to help you, as a parent,

• Recognize your sensitive child's unique temperament birthright.
• Celebrate what makes him special and convey to him the advantages of being sensitive.
• Help him cope with the challenges and difficulties of being sensitive.
• Broaden his skills and enlarge the areas in which he feels comfortable.
• Help guide him toward capable adulthood by teaching him ways to manage his own sensitivity.

If your child's individuality is a loom, with half the threads present from birth, it is a loom on which you, as parents, weave experiences and attitudes and memories into those fundamental biological threads. This book is about the warp and weft of your sensitive child's personality, and your role in creating that tapestry.

◆ 2 ◆

The Origins of Sensitivity:
How Biology and Experience Shape
Temperament

Just as wise parents have always known that
children arrive in the world endowed with their
own unique personalities, philosophers and scientists over the centuries have observed these differences and struggled to explain them.

Humans have been studying temperament as
long as there have been human beings. People have
been scrutinizing the personality quirks of their
neighbors as long as there have been neighbors to
scrutinize. Why, we wonder, is one neighbor consistently angry and vengeful, while another is easygoing, sociable, and cheerful? Why do two sisters
respond so differently to poverty or misfortune;
one is crushed, and the other manages to cope and
thrive despite adversity?

These are old questions, and for thousands of
years we have hungered for explanations. Because
of that hunger, we have occasionally swallowed explanations that have not withstood the test of time.

Today, however, we have more means than ever for finding and evaluating answers.

A SHORT HISTORY OF TEMPERAMENT

The history of our understanding of human personality and temperament is not one of unalloyed progress. Some views that once held sway seem silly to us today, and those we hold today may well be modified in time. Throughout history, the pendulum has swung back and forth between an emphasis on biology to an emphasis on environment. And with each swing of the pendulum, some sound concepts may be cast out along with invalid ones.

The Classical View

In Western civilization, attitudes toward temperament were shaped for millenia by the classical views of the Greeks. The ancient physicians Hippocrates and Galen classified the array of human personalities in terms of "humours"—fluids within the body that, when properly balanced, yielded the ideal well-adjusted personality. Imbalances, in the form of an excess of one of these four humours, produced specific temperamental extremes.

In this view, the sanguine person, governed by the influence of blood, was cheerful and outgoing (much like the extroverted, energetic "people person" of today).

The choleric type, influenced by an excess of choler, or "yellow bile," was aggressive and easily angered.

The phlegmatic person (influenced by phlegm, or, in later centuries, lymph), was stoic, calm, and self-possessed.

And finally, the melancholic temperament was created by an excess of black bile, yielding a shy, sad, introverted sort.

The idea that body fluids control personality may seem quaint today, but the influence of these categories endured in the Western world well into the eighteenth century. Even today, we allude to them when we refer to someone whose outlook is sanguine or melancholic or bilious or phlegmatic. And we still talk of the hot blood of the passionate, and the cold blood of the merciless.

With the flourishing of science and philosophy during the Enlightenment, however, these views finally became subject to closer scrutiny. Advances in medicine and anatomy opened up an interest in the structure of the brain and nervous system. New philosophical and political views championed ideas of human freedom and social and political opportunity. The classical approach to human nature began to seem rigid and limiting.

The Uses and Misuses of Science

By the 1800s, science dominated the study of temperament. New theories and explanations of human nature arose from discoveries in anatomy, archeology, genetics, and evolution. Investigators eagerly looked beyond blood and bile to study the relative size of brain structures, the structure of the skeleton, the shape of the head, the pigmentation of the skin.

The hidden mysteries of temperament, personality, and even virtue, it was believed, had to leave some physical evidence on the human body. And so scientists went to work with scales, calipers, charts, and graphs, hoping to detect disease, measure intelligence, determine personality, predict criminal behavior, and assess character.

By the early twentieth century, the Eugenics movement championed these approaches as a way of improving humankind by defining "ideal" types, restricting the immigration of "inferior" types, and discouraging reproduction among people defined as retarded, criminal, or mentally ill.

Not surprisingly, the "ideal" human being always seemed to bear a remarkable resemblance to the people doing the defining. And—again, not surprisingly—the excesses of the Eugenics movement were enthusiastically embraced by political leaders with agendas of their own.

By the 1930s, fascist leaders were proclaiming the

superiority of the Aryan "ideal" specimen and the scientifically provable "inferiority" of other types. After World War II, the world was so repelled by the implications of biological evaluations of human traits that the scientific community turned away from most research into temperament.

Psychological Views of Temperament

At the same time, psychiatrists, psychologists, and other researchers were looking at other sources of explanation for human behavior in all its variety. During the same decades that the Eugenics movement was concentrating on biological differences, psychology was looking closely at the influence of the environment on personality.

Behaviorists, influenced by the pioneering work of Ivan Pavlov, argued that behavior was learned, not innate. It was, they said, molded by early childhood experience, not by inborn balances of fluids, inherited body shape, or head bumps.

According to this view, children behave in certain ways not because of innate physical differences, but in response to rewards and punishments, positive and negative experiences. Thus, the shy, sensitive child is shy because she has, early in life, learned to associate strangers or new social experiences with unpleasant sensations.

The behaviorist view meshed well with progressive social policies that encouraged universal education and universal suffrage. After all, according to this view, any child, whatever her economic condition or ethnic heritage, could be raised to succeed in life.

Sigmund Freud, as well, promoted the idea that experience, rather than physical differences, molded personality. Freud, however, concentrated on the lingering effects of early childhood experiences; thus, an adult might be anxious, fearful, or neurotic because of some traumatic experience or unresolved guilt. Freudians might view a shy little boy as fearful because of unresolved anger at his father.

Psychologists today argue about the validity of many of Freud's insights, but his contributions to our understanding of the role of the subconscious remain significant. Most modern psychologists agree that much of our emotional experience takes place in areas over which we have little conscious control. Whether we discuss this realm in terms of the id and ego, or whether we refer to the anatomical structures of the brain's primitive limbic system, we are acknowledging the fundamental role that emotion and feeling play in guiding our thoughts and our lives.

In the 1920s the Swiss psychologist Carl Jung outlined his view of the essential differences in human personality types in terms that are still useful. He described two basic types: the introvert, who by nature draws inward, away from the activity of the world; and the extrovert, who is outward-looking, and eager to act upon the physical world.

Jung's basic types were further broken down into

subcategories based on how people perceive the world. Thus, both introverts and extroverts could approach life either emotionally or intellectually, intuitively or literally.

Sensitivity is clearly associated with Jung's introvert, especially when the sensitivity has to do with social interactions. However, some of the kinds of sensitivity discussed in this book might well be found in extroverted people. Many emotionally sensitive children, for example, are also social and outgoing.

Psychological explanations of personality and temperament that emphasized early childhood experience have implications that are both liberating and burdensome.

On one hand is the uplifting idea that any child has the potential to thrive, as long as the environment is nurturing and sound.

But if a child does become deeply troubled—shy to the point of complete isolation, neurotic, compulsive, or delinquent—this view makes it easy to place "blame" on the environment. Emotional illness or personality difficulties may be blamed on parents, and usually the mother takes the brunt of this blame.

A New Balance: Biology Reexamined

In the past few decades, our understanding of temperament has blossomed, in part because researchers have felt freer to examine biological explanations. At the same time, newly discovered ways of measuring behavior, tracking the actions of genes, and imaging the structure and activity of the brain have opened up exciting new avenues for research.

During this century, serious research into human behavior has focused on the interaction between biologically determined traits and the environment in which we grow: the time-honored balance between nature and nurture.

MEASURING SENSITIVITY

Researchers who study temperament use a variety of techniques to make sure they are looking at innate temperament, rather than behavior that is learned or influenced by a changing environment.

It's harder to observe and measure temperament as clearly and objectively as we do other innate qualities, like eye color or head shape. It's hard to say whether a particular child is shy because of her genes, or because she had a scary experience last year, or even if she's just acting shy today because she didn't get enough sleep last night.

So researchers observe the behavior of children in different situations to measure energy level, inhibition, willingness to approach, fearfulness, and other traits. The amount of time it takes a child to leave her mother's side in a new setting may be used as a measure of inhibition. The speed with which a child darts from one activity to another may track energy, activity level, or even the need for novelty and adventure. Some researchers have devised a "fidgetometer" to measure squirming in babies.

Psychologist and child development expert Jerome Kagan and his associates have conducted many of the studies that define and measure inhibited, or as he calls it, reactive behavior in children.

In one study, fourteen-month-olds were observed as they and their mothers played in a laboratory setting. From time to time a researcher unknown to the children would enter the room, or might ask the child to approach an unfamiliar toy, or speak to the child in varying tones of voice. Some children responded to these mildly disconcerting experiences with enthusiasm and confidence, while others showed distress.

Markers of inhibition included longer time spent at the mother's side, crying at the sight of the unfamiliar adult, refusal to approach or to play with the toys, and refusal to speak to the stranger.

The definition of inhibition was not limited to the observable behavior of the children. The researchers also measured the children's heart rate, blood pressure, and saliva levels of cortisol, making a link between inhibited behavior and biological functions: variable heart rate and blood pressure that increased in "fear" provoking situations, and higher levels of cortisol (produced by the adrenal gland) were seen as markers of inhibited temperament.

These observations of the behavior of children

actually mesh with new discoveries in brain science. We now know a great deal about how brain chemicals known as neurotransmitters are produced and received, and how they are transformed or buffered by other chemicals. We know more about how medications can alter or improve mood. We know more about how these chemical patterns vary among individuals. Much recent research suggests that sensitive behavior is generated by a sensitive brain: A tendency to react quickly, to be cautious, to be fearful or anxious, and to react to low levels of noise or light or smell may be traceable to the sensitivity of brain structures and the connections between them.

We've made great strides not only in understanding the chemical pathways that generate sensation and consciousness, but also the differentiation of brain structure and function.

The limbic system—a cluster of structures deep within the brain—receives a stimulus and assigns a response and an emotional value: Is this stimulus pleasant? Unpleasant? Can it be ignored, or does it call for fighting or running away?

Often this assessment and response takes place before the thoughtful realm of the cerebrum has had a chance to evaluate the stimulus rationally. Thus, we see a snake and instantly recoil, before our cerebrum processes the evidence and informs us that what we see is actually the coiled garden hose.

There is still much to be learned about how different temperaments relate to brain structure and function. But there is evidence that people who are highly prone to anxiety, or who are extremely wary in unfamiliar situations, have a biological basis for this trait.

Most likely, this biological basis is centered in the degree of excitability of the limbic system. These structures control those basic responses and emotions we share with lower animals: fear, anger, alertness, sexual desire. The hippocampus, for example, distinguishes between familiar and unfamiliar stimuli and plays a role in the memory of emotions. If it detects an unfamiliar, or unpleasant, stimulus, it stimulates the nearby amygdala, which regulates the fear response. These are primitive structures with primitive functions, yet they are taking place in humans every time a small child reacts with fear to a new face, a new place, or a new situation.

Despite the term "slow-to-warm-up," sensitive children who exhibit that trait probably have very quick, acute reactions, neurologically speaking. The hippocampus, amygdala, and related structures may be more excitable and easily stimulated in these children than in others.

These inhibited children show various physiological traits: They have higher levels of cortisol in saliva and higher heart rates and diastolic blood pressure. Their facial expression mirrors the wary, anxious look that animals also exhibit when threatened.

Other aspects of sensitivity may also have a biological underpinning. Children who are sensitive to odors may have higher levels of the brain chemical norepinephrine, which heightens the sensitivity of receptors in the olfactory region of the brain.

SENSITIVITY AND GENES

Most definitions of temperament include the element of heritability. They assume a genetic basis for human variation in behavior, but evidence is difficult to come by. No one has yet identified a "shy gene," or a "fussy gene," or a "can't sit still gene." We can't track and identify these traits by selectively breeding humans for certain qualities, the way we do with dogs.

One approach is to sort out genetic from environmental influences by studying twins, who offer a unique window into the workings of biology and environment.

Several studies have examined groups of twins, observed their behavior and temperament, and then compared the way sets of identical twins differ from pairs of fraternal twins. This distinction is key to studying how much of a trait may be explained by genes.

Identical, or monozygotic, twins come from one egg that divides after fertilization; and thus share the same genetic material. Fraternal, or dizygotic, twins are the result of the fertilization of two eggs by two sperm. Thus, although they share the same intrauterine environment and the same birthday, fraternal twins are no more alike than any two siblings.

In twin studies of behavior, researchers observe groups of identical twins and compare their behavior to groups of fraternal twins. Since all identical twins are same-sex, they are matched with same-sex fraternal twin pairs in these studies.

These experiments also control for environmental influences by studying twin pairs who are being raised together in normal families, so each child has essentially the same life experiences as the other. If the identical twin pairs show more similarity to each other than the fraternal twins do, the differences are very likely genetic.

The Institute for Behavioral Genetics at the University of Colorado has been conducting a longitudinal study of this type, measuring inhibited, fearful behavior in toddler twins. Investigators tracked children's willingness to leave the mother in an unfamiliar setting, to approach a stranger, and to play with an unfamiliar toy. Comparing the behavior of identical to fraternal twins, researchers concluded that shared heredity accounted for at least half of the observed behavior.

It's important to point out that these figures do not point to a particular gene, or easily identified genetic trait that produces shyness or sensitivity in a child. It does suggest, however, that the entire spectrum of biological traits has combined to provide the child with a predisposition toward cautious or reactive behavior.

Even when the hereditory explanation of a particular behavior is strong, it is never total. There is still a significant part of any child's temperament that has explanations other than genetics, and that is the realm of environment, early childhood experience, and the wisdom and skills of parents.

SENSITIVITY AND SURVIVAL

If temperament has a genetic basis, it must have some survival value. It's easy to imagine the value of a bold, aggressive, forceful temperament in prehistoric times, especially in the effort to hunt for food and vanquish enemies. And a trait like adaptability—the ability to adjust to new situations or even to seek out and embrace the unfamiliar—certainly could contribute to survival.

But so might the quieter traits, like sensitivity. Being shy may seem a handicap in the contemporary world, but in prehistoric times, the prudent, wary human would have advantages over her bold neighbor.

Similarly, acute hearing, the ability to detect unusual flavors, a tendency to startle easily, even a tendency among the young to "freeze" in dangerous situations all have survival value.

Sensitive children often have a prolonged "freezing" reaction when confronted by new people or situations. This response to a potential threat has its correlates in the animal world: baby rabbits freeze when predators are near; monkeys respond to unfamiliar animals or situations by staring quietly. Similarly, baby humans stop playing and stare quietly at strangers before responding.

Those members of a prehistoric group who possessed sensitivity may have been the "canaries" of the Stone Age coal mine. No doubt their heightened alertness and tendency to worry did not always bear fruit, but in real emergencies, they may have sensed danger or threat before others and saved the day.

SENSITIVITY IS NOT DESTINY

As intriguing as the biological discoveries about temperament may be, they still are only part of the story. If we put too much emphasis on either biology or environment, we run the risk of overlooking the subtle, complex ways these realms interact with each other.

If we overemphasize biological explanations, we risk viewing our children's personalities fatalistically, of assuming that temperament is destiny and beyond our influence as parents. And that view might prevent us from helping our children broaden their skills, their abilities, and their confidence.

If, on the other hand, we ignore the biological roots of temperament, attributing all aspects of personality to environment, we may be tempted to try to change or "cure" qualities that are innate; qualities that have inherent worth.

And if our children disappoint us or develop problems, we as parents can become burdened with guilt, agonizing over what we might have done to traumatize our child so much that she clings fearfully to us at the kindergarten doorway.

Ultimately, however, biology and environmental influence are so closely woven together that it's exceedingly difficult to sort out. We vary in the minute details of how our brains are "wired," in our production of hormones that either promote or inhibit a feeling or an action. Yet these details are not the totality of personality. They form a framework on which to hang our unique life experiences.

If a child is born with a tendency to be uncomfortable in new situations, and then many of those new experiences are unpleasant, her initial wariness will be reinforced.

If she gets a chance to learn that some experiences turn out to be worth the initial discomfort, then she will learn to manage her wariness.

The totality of the influence of nature and nurture on personality has been described as a gray fabric, with the black threads of the warp representing the biological underpinnings, and the white weft threads representing the experience built upon it. The fabric as a whole is neither white nor black, but gray.

Sensitivity really means a bias toward certain kinds of behavior—a tendency to be wary, for example, or to be aware of lower levels of stimulus than other people. It means being more comfortable in some situations than in others. Your sensitive child may be more comfortable in small groups than in large crowds, but that doesn't mean that she won't or can't function well in a large group when she needs to.

It all depends on how her family brings her up, comforts her, sets limits, prepares her for difficult situations, and talks to her about her weaknesses and her strengths.

Your child's temperament may be established at birth, but it interacts over time with a stream of experiences that build her personality. So a child may be born with an excitable amygdala that heightens her ability to experience fear. She may process information through her hippocampus in ways that warn her to watch out for a novel situation. She may be predisposed to react to sounds more intensely than other children.

And genes can affect our behavior in roundabout ways. Certain temperaments may lead us to select certain environments; we may gravitate toward realms in which we feel temperamentally comfortable. Shy children may withdraw from the kinds of group activities that might help them learn more social skills; adults who are uncomfortable with change and novelty may seek careers in which they may perform predictable, orderly tasks.

So the link between nature and nurture is complex and circular. And the conclusion must be that despite the fundamental importance of temperament, sensitivity is *not* destiny. Rather, it is a bias toward certain behaviors, a style of behavior that feels comfortable to a particular child. It is not fate, and neither is it an assemblage of superficial habits and quirks. Rather, it is a birthright.

◆ 3 ◆

The Challenge:
Why Raising a Sensitive Child Is So Hard

"I have logged more time at children's birthday parties than Bozo the Clown. When we're dropping our children off at a party, all the other parents leave, and come back later to pick up their children. I'm the only mother who has to stay. Corey absolutely will not stay without me. I hate having to do this, but if I don't, she'll have even less chance to interact with other children."

"Alexis is the easiest child in the world to discipline—*too* easy! We have to be very gentle with any kind of criticism—she cries if we so much as look at her funny. I'm really worried about next year, when she'll be in second grade. I'm afraid she'll get Mrs. Price, who *yells* at the kids. She's really a very nice teacher; that's just her style. Most of the kids just roll with it. But Alexis will be devastated!"

"I'm ready to give up. I simply can't understand what makes Chad tick. I'm trying to get him to sleep through the night and be less fearful, but it seems that everything I try goes nowhere. I feel completely powerless."

"Dealing with James's behavior has worn me down. Everything we do turns into a battle. Just the simplest things, like picking out what he's going to wear, or getting him to put on a hat when it's freezing outside. He's so negative, it's as though he has it in for me."

Four sensitive children, four stressed-out parents. Embarrassment, worry, fatigue—they come with the territory for all parents, from time to time, but to the parents of sensitive children, in particular. We rejoice when our chidren are joyous, and we ache when they are in pain. Our sensitive children seem to us to be venturing out into a cold, threatening world like little hermit crabs without their shells. How will they ever survive? How can we keep them safe and happy?

Often, the worries and frustrations of parents like the ones quoted above grow out of an inability to understand what the sensitive child is feeling. As we discuss below, rapport between a parent and child's temperaments is something that does not always come naturally.

But also, parents worry because they remember pain, worry, and missed opportunities from their own childhoods. Your sensitive child is not sensitive in a vacuum. You, as his parents, share his triumphs and his troubles, tear your hair over his balkiness, or agonize over his hurt feelings.

Part of what's difficult about being the parent of a sensitive child is practical: how to get your child to join the other children at the playground, to try new foods, to let go of your leg at the nursery school doorway.

But parents of sensitive children have questions and concerns that go much deeper. Here are some typical ones:

- What makes my child tick? Why is he so different from me? He's begging for us to bring him home from camp. I *loved* camp.
- Have I failed my child? What did I do wrong? Did I traumatize her when she was a baby? Did I go back to work too soon? Should I have breast-fed? Should we have paid for private school?
- How can I meet the needs of my sensitive child without shortchanging my other children who aren't as sensitive?
- What's going to become of my sensitive child when he grows up? Will he ever have friends? How on earth will he ever ask a girl for a date? Will he be a hermit? How will he handle rejection? How will he survive a job interview?
- How will I help my shy, withdrawn child develop "street smarts"?
- My child seems out of step with the world. Entertainment, social interactions, athletics, are all

geared toward the child who joins in, competes, speaks up, and enjoys excitement, and my child prefers to sit by himself and draw.

- Even when I understand my child, how do I explain him to other people who don't? How do I protect my child from other people who say, "But he's so shy!"

"She'll be fine after you leave. The only way to get her to stop crying is to just turn and walk away."

"In *my* family, the children eat what I serve or they don't eat at all!"

"Oh, he'll get used to Attila. How will he ever learn to like dogs if you're so protective? Here, Attila! Come and make friends with Michael!"

SENSITIVITY AND YOUR OWN HISTORY

Raising a sensitive child can be a delightful experience, because sensitive children can themselves be delightful. That's especially true when parents have managed to separate their own agenda, and their own pleasant and unpleasant memories of childhood, from the needs of their child.

We all experienced sensitivity as children, whether we were sensitive ourselves or had a sensitive family member or friend. We have grown up with attitudes toward shyness, fear, anxiety, fussiness, and any number of temperament-based behaviors. It's wise to take a moment and review our own memories and attitudes toward sensitivity before we get busy with the task of helping our own children.

Which of the following statements are true for you or your spouse?

1. I remember vividly the absolute panic I felt on my first day of kindergarten.
2. It was very difficult for me to make friends. I felt so alone, and I don't want my child to experience that loneliness.
3. I remember how hurt I was when I was picked last for the basketball team.
4. I remember how much I dreaded giving oral reports in school.
5. I still dread oral reports—even though it's my *child* who's giving them.
6. When my little brother and I played, I had to let him win all the time. If he lost, he would get so upset that my mother punished *me*.
7. You don't do children any favors by indulging their fears. My parents made me conquer my fears by being tough, and my kids can do the same.
8. My parents demanded the best from me. They didn't hesitate to point out my faults or those of others.
9. My parents were too strict, and I'm determined not to repeat their mistakes.
10. My parents let me get away with murder, and I'm determined not to repeat their mistakes.

If you're able to answer any of these questions in the affirmative, you'll see that issues of sensitivity don't begin with the birth of your sensitive child. Whether you are sensitive or not, your own childhood hovers over every aspect of your life as a parent.

Whether our own temperaments are sensitive or otherwise, we all, as parents, share the desire to see our children grow up happy. Sometimes that means we want them to enjoy what *we* enjoyed as children, other times to be spared what we suffered as kids.

The key to raising your sensitive child is to empathize, but to empathize *appropriately*. That means that if you suffered from sensitivity, and see your child doing the same, you need to respond to your child's experiences in an adult way, rather than as the hurt child you remember being.

THE IMPORTANCE OF FIT

Just as children are born with different temperaments, so were their parents. Despite the degree of genetic foundation for temperament, children do not necessarily have the same temperament as their parents, any more than they have the same color hair or the same talent for art, music, or gymnastics.

And so, inevitably, sensitive children are born into not-so-sensitive families.

When parent and child seem to be at one another's throats in every thing they do, when temperaments don't mesh, parents can be baffled, frustrated, disappointed, guilty. Parents who don't share their child's sensitivity can, despite the best of intentions, make the situation worse (more on this in Chapter Five).

Let's look at the categories of sensitivity described in Chapter One and see how the mixes or matches of temperament can play out in family relationships.

Low Sensory Threshold

Sarah's mother dreads winter. Not because of the cold or the heating bills, but because of winter clothing. Five-year-old Sarah loves the snow and waits for it eagerly. But when other children jump into their snowsuits and rush out the door, Sarah is like a temperamental Parisian chef. She asks for a particular pair of socks, because the new ones are too bunchy on her toes. Then the mittens itch. The fastening on the boots are too tight, or too loose.

Once Sarah and her mother have leaped all these hurdles and have made it out the door, she plays contentedly for five minutes. Then snow gets into the tops of her boots, melts against her ankles, and Sarah begins to wail.

Sarah is genuinely bothered by the sensations she feels on her skin, including temperature, texture, and mild discomforts that would never keep another child indoors on a zesty winter day. Fortunately, her mother, too, has a low threshold, and is understanding and patient.

When a sensitive child and her parents share this style of sensitivity, there's a natural rapport and, usually, few problems. The household may be quieter than some, entertainment calmer, even foods more bland. When the sensitive child complains that her shoes pinch, her parents are likely to understand and make efforts to make her comfortable.

There may be problems, however, if both parent and child are so comfortable with their low-stimulus environment that the parent makes no effort to help the sensitive child widen her comfort zone so that she can feel at ease in other homes and in other settings. Fortunately for Sarah, although her mother tries to make her comfortable, she does encourage her to participate.

If, however, the sensitive child has parents with high threshold for stimuli, it can be difficult for everyone.

A child who refuses to wear his jacket unless the temperature drops below freezing is likely to face strong disapproval from a parent who doesn't understand that he feels too warm in the jacket.

Other children are particular about their possessions or their clothing in ways that baffle their less sensitive parents. Robert, who is four, demands that his shoes be tied in just such a way that the ends of the laces do not, repeat, not, touch the floor. If one end of the lace touches the floor, Robert is upset and begs to have them retied.

Robert is particular in other areas, too. When he

prepares to draw, he gets out his coloring books and box of crayons, proceeds to take out one color, use it, then return it to the box before extracting another crayon. His parents are pleased that he is so tidy, but baffled by his compulsiveness.

And then there's Eric. He feels every grain of sand in his shoe, every scratchy label inside his clothing. If there's a mosquito within a mile, it locates and bites Eric, ignoring less flavorful prey.

Eric's parents and his older sisters love to go camping. To them, trudging along wilderness trails surrounded by the beauty of nature is heaven itself. They can't understand why Eric should be so negative about the outdoors. Eric's father thinks his son is a whiner who needs to be toughened up. He is convinced that going easy on Eric will only make the situation worse, so he is relentless in his insistence that Eric keep up physically, and he is dismissive of Eric's complaints.

Social Sensitivity

As with sensory threshold, parents and child who are both socially sensitive have a good rapport.

However, social skills in any child—sensitive or otherwise—do not come naturally. They must be accumulated through experience and guidance. The drawback of this kind of meshing of parent and child's style is that sensitive parents may not think to help expand their child's skills. It isn't enough for the child to be happy and comfortable; he needs to gently broaden his abilities as well.

However, the more challenging situation is one in which a sensitive child is shy or prefers solitude, and lives in a family full of bustling social activity. In this situation, exasperated parents often pressure the shy child to participate and, in so doing, increase the shyness.

One adult sensitive child recalls how frustrated she felt growing up with a mother who had been the belle of the ball in high school.

"My mother was very popular and dated a lot. She'd been a class officer and on all sorts of committees, and she would tell me over and over about all this. I felt like such a failure because I was never elected to anything and didn't feel comfortable around boys. I felt that because I didn't date, I was somehow failing my family."

This woman now realizes that her mother was probably trying, in her own way, to help her quiet daughter. She was saying, in essence, "See how much fun I had? You can, too, if you'll just make the effort." Yet her comments had the opposite effect.

Emotional Sensitivity

When parent and child are both emotionally reactive, again, there may be rapport. But there are drawbacks to this combination. A family with an anxious, worried parent and a sensitive child may develop into a crucible of intense emotion that has a hard time finding release. Everyone walks on eggshells, everyone hurts each other's feelings.

Suppose, for example, the mother is worried about keeping her job. Most parents are able to manage these adult worries without overburdening a small child, but an emotionally sensitive mother may obsess about her worries. She may bring home endless discussions about the nuances of office politics to be discussed over dinner. She may talk endlessly about worst-case scenarios and walk around with a worried face.

Her emotionally sensitive daughter may find the anxiety devastating. Not only is she worried about her mother and worried about the future, she can't easily turn to her mother for comfort.

Or, the same emotional combination can cause family members to retreat into tense silence. The anxieties are there, picked up by the alert child, but they are not explicitly discussed.

When the parents are emotionally thick-skinned and the child is tender, however, the consequences can be difficult as well. A child in this situation may seem to be a complainer without a cause. Parents may pooh-pooh the child's feelings, disparage him for them, and pressure him to relinquish those feelings.

This is especially true when the child is fearful of something that, according to conventional wisdom, isn't scary: swimming in the deep end, fireworks, loud music. Parents—with the best of intentions—may try to force the child to get past this nonsensical fear.

In these families, battle lines are easily drawn between the anxious child and the parents, who feel the need to push the child into actions which may frighten him, and to "get over" the worry.

Emotionally sensitive children are particularly susceptible to reprimands. What might seem to the parent to be a mild criticism can seem devastating to the child. Over time, such children may develop powerful feelings of shame and guilt.

Similarly, emotionally sensitive children may not seem able to tolerate ordinary teasing that other children take in stride. They may even take minor jokes literally, mystifying their elders.

At a family gathering, six-year-old Katie asked her aunt and uncle what would be served for dinner. Katie's uncle said, "I think we'll have penguin stew with squid sauce." The other children giggled, but Katie became agitated.

"Mom!" she cried. "Uncle Jeff says we're having penguin stew for dinner. We're not *really* having penguin, are we, Mom? Mom?"

Sensitivity to Change

After a day at the shore, five-year-old Amanda and her parents stopped at a small amusement part on the boardwalk. It was evening, and the rides were beginning to close down. One ride, with little cars shaped like zoo animals that swung around from chains appealed to Amanda and she begged to have a ride. After some discussion, Amanda's parents persuaded the man to open the ride again for Amanda.

Suddenly, just as she was being helped into a car shaped like an elephant, Amanda began to protest. The carnival man tried to encourage her. But Amanda refused.

A different parent, one who did not share her temperament, might have pressured Amanda to go on the ride, or chastised her for inconveniencing the family and the carnival worker. But Amanda's mother, who, like her, is sensitive to new situations, recalls, "I understood that suddenly she realized it was scary. But that was okay. Even though we'd gone to the trouble of getting the man to open up the ride, and then Amanda refused, it was not an issue."

Ever since she was born, Lori was fussy, wakeful, and easily distressed. Her mother found it enormously frustrating to try to get Lori up and dressed and off to day care, and then take her on errands after work and on weekends. Lori's older brother had rolled with the punches, but Lori fussed at every change.

A parent who shared Lori's difficulty with novelty and transition would understand, and adjust the family's schedule and commitments to ease her way. But Lori's mother gets restless and bored when there isn't a lot going on. It's difficult for her to understand what's bothering her daughter, and equally difficult to adjust to a slower pace. So she keeps trying to amuse Lori, taking her to parks and zoos and friends' homes, hoping to please her. And the more she tries, the more unhappy Lori is.

Certainly, the most challenging situations occur when temperaments clash, because less sensitive parents have a difficult time understanding their child.

But similar temperaments are not necessarily without problems either. No matter how comfortable the child is in his home situation, he needs to gird his loins and leave the nest with adequate skills.

And it's when parent and child are very much alike that it's sometimes hardest for parents to let go of their own burden of childhood memories about being sensitive. If the child is hurt in the same way that the parent remembers being hurt, the pain for both is intense.

But ultimately, any combination of temperaments can work well for the child, because fit is something that is forged by the family.

In child development circles, the term "fit" is not limited to the degree to which parent and child temperaments match. Parents and children often differ, and yet manage well. What is usually referred to is the relationship that parent and child build, a workable and livable fit between parental expectations and the child's abilities. And that, ultimately, is what you, as the parent of a sensitive child, will be working toward. Whatever the match or mismatch between your temperament and that of your child, you can create a fit and rapport that works.

THE SENSITIVE BOY

When the sensitive child is a girl, life is a bit easier because traditional gender-based expectations are more in keeping with her temperament. But boys have a difficult time. Even today, there's considerable pressure on little boys to be tough, or, if they're not tough, to act tough. Eric's backpacking father finds it doubly frustrating that the non-rugged child in his family is his son, rather than his daughter.

The kinds of sensitivity that cause the most difficulty for boys are low sensory threshold and emotional sensitivity. A boy who is particular about clothing or aromas, or one who bursts into tears easily, runs the risk of feeling out of step and even scorned, while his similarly sensitive sister might be accepted, or even admired. A socially sensitive boy who dislikes parties or prefers to play by himself, on the other hand, has a style that meshes more easily with masculine roles.

A father, in particular, may feel edgy about having a sensitive son and may feel that his son's behavior reflects on his own masculinity, or on his effectiveness in bringing up his boy properly.

One of the most challenging temperament combinations can be a sensitive father who has painful memories of not measuring up in his own childhood, and a son who, in the father's eyes, shows some of the same "inadequacies" such as tenderness of emotion or lack of physical robustness. For specifics on dealing with this combination, see Chapter Six.

STRANGERS IN A STRANGE LAND

"Jason's fourth grade class sold flowers to raise money for our local homeless shelter. His group sold the most and won a class trip to a sports and entertainment center that's full of video games, batting cages, and other activities. After about twenty minutes, he called me and said he wanted to come home. He hated the crowds, the screaming kids, the flashing lights, and the pounding music. I should have known—he just can't tolerate frantic, noisy situations. He either runs around like a maniac, or he bursts into tears. To the other kids, it's heaven, but for Jason, it's sheer torture."

Jason's mother struggles on a daily basis with this sense of mismatch between her son and the pace of modern life. Although she and her son have established a good rapport, she is aware that Jason and his culture do not fit in the least.

The sensitive child is, in some ways, a victim of the vicissitudes of fashion. There was a time when timidity and delicacy were expected and admired in children. (Remember the Princess and the Pea?)

Not too many years ago, parents struggled to protect children from a range of dangers, from injury to contagious disease. In those days, caution, hesitance, and obedience were encouraged in children.

That was then. This is now.

Today's child is expected to be a bit tougher than the princess who felt the bruising effect of a pea under all those mattresses. Today we expect children to be eager and active, sturdy little soccer players, busy social butterflies, and enthusiastic participants in the talent show.

These days, we nudge children through a packed daily schedule full of activities, lessons, and sports. We entertain them with amusements that are skewed toward the manic, whether it's screeching television commercials, frenetic birthday parties, or outings at children's entertainment centers full of music, jungle gyms, and video games.

To be sure, many of today's children thrive on such a regimen. But a sizable minority have a hard time coping with the pace, the noise, the confusion, the chaos, the new faces around every corner, the constant shifting of gears.

And if the children have trouble, the parents do, too. Trying to soothe, motivate, encourage, feed, clothe, educate, and run interference for a sensitive child can be challenging indeed.

FIT AND OTHERS

The issue of fit applies to many dimensions of your child's life, and not just in your relationship to him. A poor temperament fit between your sensitive child and his brothers and sisters, for example, can make issues like family routines and discipline into major problems.

And your child's relationship with other family members can create the potential for poor fit (as with aunts and uncles who feel compelled to point out how shy your child is).

The same is true of your child's teacher, camp counselor, or other authority figure.

Alexis's mother, quoted at the beginning of this chapter, knows that her daughter and Mrs. Price don't have good rapport. Mrs. Price may mean well. Her loud, emotionally up-front approach to classroom discipline may be appropriate for energetic, hard-to-manage children. But it's not suitable to Alexis's needs. For more on dealing with your sensitive child and school situations, see Chapter Eight.

This dissonance crops up in many interactions, even casual ones. One mother—whose child is decidedly *not* sensitive—volunteered at her son's school and was struck by the difference between her own son and some of the other children in his classroom.

She had volunteered to help out in David's fourth grade class during their weekly visit to the school's computer room. The class spent an hour a week learning how to use the keyboard and play simple games and learning programs.

In this case, it was several of the other children in the class, not her son, who were sensitive. David is a boisterous, leap-before-you-look boy, and Laura dreaded the prospect of being responsible for twenty five Davids in a room filled with expensive equipment.

"There I was," Laura recalls, "gearing up to use my drill sergeant voice, the way I have to with David. But here were these children, paying attention, and looking at all the instructions before they'd even touch a key. One little girl kept looking up at me for permission before she'd do anything. Their fingers were so careful and gentle on the keyboards. David, of course, was pounding away on his, as usual.

"After a while I realized that a lot of the children were scared of me when I used my loud, serious voice. These quieter, more careful children didn't need that. I had to find a new way of relating to them."

FIT AS A TWO-WAY STREET

As David's mother is learning, the temperament of a child can influence the behavior of a parent, just as parental behavior influences a child. Parents certainly teach their children, but children teach parents and other adults, too. We are not fated to remain locked into a temperament dynamic that isn't working, whether it's different temperaments that don't mesh well, or identical temperaments that don't allow enough growth. What parents can do is learn to understand their child's temperament and adjust their parenting style to accommodate it.

Your sensitive child's temperament has helped form the kind of parent you are. If your child is challenging, the chances are that it's not your "fault"; rather, it's probably a combination of his temperament, your own, and the specifics of your child-management approach. You can't do much about temperament, but you can find better ways to manage the challenging aspects of temperament.

While it's difficult to raise a sensitive child, it's also challenging to *be* one. Parents who understand the challenges their sensitive child is facing will be better able to establish rapport. We'll discuss what sensitivity feels like in Chapter Four.

◈ 4 ◈

A View From the Inside: What Being Sensitive Feels Like

Too often, the behavior of the sensitive child is defined by people on the outside looking in. The outsider sees fear, when the sensitive child sees herself as exercising a reasonable caution. The outsider sees snobbishness, when the socially sensitive adult sees herself as needing her own space. The outsider sees laziness, when the sensitive person sees herself as savoring life's small moments.

Five-year-old-Ryan and his uncle are at the indoor party center, where there's a wonderful multilevel play area full of tubes, rope webs for climbing, and pits full of colored plastic balls to romp in. The whole area is vibrating with noisy, scampering children.

Ryan's uncle invites him to jump into the plastic balls. Ryan hesitates, and his uncle says, "Come on, Sport! Go on! Have fun!" Of course Ryan wants to have fun. But what lies in front of him doesn't look the least bit fun—unbearable noise that he can't process, movement and actions that he can't predict, large, fast-moving children, the possibility of getting kicked or stepped on, or getting lost under all those bright blue balls—how deep is it, anyway? To Ryan, it looks like as much fun as diving into a vat full of alligators.

Hannah, who is seven, is having dinner at her grandparents' house. Her parents have instructed her to eat what she is served and not complain about the food. But her grandmother is serving asparagus. Hannah wants very much to cooperate, but she knows that the texture of asparagus makes her gag. She wonders if she should try to eat it anyway, or refuse and risk disapproval.

Matthew is in an enchanted realm. It started out as a simple kaleidoscope on his shelf. He picked it up and held it up toward his window, where the morning sun made the colored glass patterns glow with an otherworldly splendor. As the shapes transform themselves before his eyes, Matthew hears a faint voice in the distance. He brushes it aside so he can continue his reverie. The voice keeps trying to drag him back into the colorless, mundane world. It is saying, "Aren't you dressed yet? Will you stop *dawdling* and get *going*? We're going to be late!"

As the parent of a sensitive child, you need to "try on" her sensitivity, to go beyond what her sensitivity looks like to you, and gain an understanding of what it feels like to her.

This empathy is especially important if you and your child have dramatically different temperaments. If you are naturally social, it may take an effort to understand your child's preference for solitude, or for small, intimate gatherings of friends rather than huge parties.

If you can accomplish this, you will be less likely to misdiagnose your child's behavior. Your task as a parent of a sensitive child is to understand sensitivity, and to help your child define it in positive terms and manage its challenging aspects. These tasks require that you understand what it feels like to be sensitive.

And until these tasks are accomplished, parents run the risk of misunderstanding their children, misinterpreting their behavior, and missing opportunities for helping their children grow and thrive.

Pitfalls of Not Understanding Sensitivity

- You misdiagnose behavior. You say she's being defiant when she's desperate. You say she's being lazy when she's preoccupied. You say she's whining when she's trying to get help easing her discomfort.
- You develop a victim mentality. You begin to talk yourself into powerless parenting behavior. "Whatever I do, it's wrong. No matter what I try,

I can't seem to get her to (call a friend, wear her new coat, eat her vegetables)."

- You deny her real perceptions. "You are not scared. That's not scary at all. Don't be silly." Your sensitive child knows if her feet hurt. She knows if something tastes funny, and she knows if the witch in the movie scares her. These are her perceptions, not yours.

- You run the risk of making your child's core identity into a negative:

    "I can't understand why you won't try out for the talent show. You're a good singer. Why won't you make the effort?"

    "Do you have to be so picky?"

    "Oh, quit whining."

    "What are you fussing about *now?*"

    "Can't you ever . . ."

- You impose your own idea of comfort on your child. If picking up the telephone and calling an acquaintance is as natural as breathing for you, it's difficult to understand that the same act brings a sense of dread to a socially sensitive child. Or you see your sensitive child playing by himself and think, "He's all alone! He must be lonely! Let's get a whole gang of kids over to play!"

WALKING A MILE IN SENSITIVE SHOES

The world of the sensitive child is rich and full, but it can be daunting. It is so full of flavors and sounds that it's easy to be overwhelmed. It's so fraught with emotions that it's quite possible for feelings of anxiety to get out of hand. It moves so fast and furiously, and it's full of all those people asking questions, staring, judging. So it's hardly surprising that sensitive children sometimes beat a hasty retreat from experiences the rest of the world thrives on.

Often, sensitive children have difficulty articulating how they feel. In childhood, they may be able to use words like *itchy* or *scary*, but their ability to explain their perceptions to others may not develop until adulthood. Therefore, our insights into what sensitive children feel often come from the recollections of sensitive adults.

Let's take a look at what each style of sensitivity feels like to children, and how it's recalled by adults.

Low Sensory Threshold

Sensitive children with low sensory threshold may be easily overwhelmed by visual sensations: flashing lights at a carnival, loud or varied sounds, strong smells. Other kids seem able to handle all these sensations, but sensitive children collect them, accumulate them, and seem unable to discharge them.

Some respond to this overload by becoming withdrawn and miserable. For others, however, the response is to lose control and to behave more wildly. Most of us have seen (or have) otherwise well-behaved children who get so worked up at birthday parties or playgrounds that they are transformed into wild beasts.

Some children with low sensory threshold have trouble making judgments between competing sensations. In school, for example, they may have trouble sorting out the teacher's words (important) from the words of other pupils whispering behind them (unimportant), or other kids laughing in the halls. Like someone trying to distinguish between the image and the background in an optical illusion, these children become easily confused in a setting with too many stimuli.

For still others, the challenge is flavors, aromas, or temperature.

Erica, age six, fidgets in the car. She's always trying to struggle out of her sweater, or complaining that it's too cold, or playing with the car windows. Her parents grumble and complain about how much she grumbles and complains. But when it's too cold, Erica feels as though she is exposed on a wintry mountaintop; when it's hot, she feels trapped in her clothing, imprisoned in the stifling car with no escape. Who *wouldn't* complain a bit under those circumstances?

"Ever since I was a kid," recalls one sensitive adult, "I was bothered by the music at the mall. Not the melodies themselves, but all the different music playing at the same time. I'd be walking down the aisle and the main part of the store would be playing one kind of music, and the Juniors Department would be playing something else. My brain couldn't just listen to one; it was so jarring that I would get tired and upset, and I couldn't really explain what was bothering me.

"They say I'm picky. I say I'm perceptive—I notice differences that other people don't. Why should that be bad? It seems to me it's important to notice differences."

Social Sensitivity

Picture yourself as a socially sensitive child in a social gathering like a family reunion or a large picnic. Adults and children mill around, talking and laughing. People are approaching you and asking questions about school, your family, sports. All these questions require answers, and you know that there are so many chances of messing up and saying the wrong thing that you say absolutely nothing. Naturally, everyone notices; they ask why you're so quiet and shy, everyone joins in, you feel yourself blushing. Everyone laughs and points out that you're blushing, which, of course, makes you blush more.

Socially sensitive children feel acutely aware of being on stage, of having attention drawn to them.

"I distinctly remember, when I was about four, being introduced to one of my mother's friends. I had enough trouble meeting strange new people, anyway, but this woman made it even worse. She bent down and looked right in my face and said, 'Why, HellOOOOO! Aren't you aDOORable!' in this high, unnatural falsetto. Her weird voice made a strange situation even stranger, and I just hid my face. Then, of course, this woman had to say, 'Oh, she's SHYY!!!' very loudly and cheerfully. To this day I don't understand why adults behave that way to shy kids. It certainly doesn't help them overcome it—quite the contrary!"

For shy children, the world of social interaction appears complex and often baffling. The chance of doing and saying the right thing seems slim, and the possibility of making some kind of mistake seems almost unlimited.

Socially sensitive children are not always shy, as we discussed in Chapter One. Some children who seem unsociable have a genuine need for more solitude than others. Consider two siblings, one socially outgoing, the other socially sensitive.

Brandon and his sister, Sarah, have a long bus ride after school. It's well after 4 P.M. when they come in the door, and they're exhausted. Both children throw down their schoolbags and grab a snack. After sitting in her fifth grade class, then sitting some more on the school bus, Sarah can hardly hold still. She's itching to run next door to see if her friend can join her on a bike ride through the neighborhood.

Brandon has been sitting, too—in a crowded third grade classroom all day, then riding on an equally crowded, boisterous school bus. Unlike his sister, however, he can hardly wait to go up to his room, close the door, and be blissfully alone. After he closes the door, his muscles relax and tension ebbs from his body. He sits at his desk and colors with markers, thinking about the day's events. No bells ring, no classmates tease, no teacher demands. After half an hour, Brandon emerges happily from his room and heads outside to shoot baskets.

Sarah is outgoing, sociable, energized by the company of others. She refills her emotional reservoir by being around people. Long periods of solitude without someone to interact with make Sarah uncomfortable.

Brandon is socially sensitive. He's friendly enough, but he refuels emotionally by being alone.

Others might judge Brandon as a loner, or as unfriendly. Yet he's simply seeking the setting in which he feels comfortable and can refresh himself.

Emotional Sensitivity

If you are an emotionally sensitive child, you pick up on every nuance of facial expression, tension, disapproval, or fear in others. If your mother is on the telephone, you can sense from subtle changes in her voice whether she's hearing bad news or if the person on the line is making her angry. Your teacher's frown devastates you, and a careless taunt from another child festers for months.

You get caught up in a whole network of "what-ifs." "What if Mom and Dad don't come home?" "What if I get lost?" "What if that dog jumps over the fence?" "What if . . . ?"

Whenever Ian's parents go out, his brother falls asleep right after the sitter puts them to bed. But Ian lies there, staring at the ceiling, worrying that something might happen to them and they won't come home. He thinks about all the possible ways they might get hurt, or kidnapped, or killed. Then he worries about what will become of his brother and him if they really don't return. He gets so worked up he sometimes lies awake until his mother and father walk in the door.

"In school, I had drawn a detailed map of South America and I was really proud of it. The teacher was going around the room, looking at everyone's work. She was looking over my shoulder and telling me what a great job I'd done. Then she pointed out that I had left out Tierra del Fuego. Her comment was kind, and it was perfectly reasonable; after all, I really needed to put Tierra del Fuego on my map. But to me, that was like a huge insult, an attack. I felt just awful, as though the whole project was worthless because she pointed out one little problem I needed to correct."

"When I was about five my uncle lifted me up to put me on the back of his horse. I'm sure he was holding on to me, but I felt terribly unstable, and I was sure I'd fall off. It was such a long way down.

And then the horse started walking—very slowly, I'm sure—and I was absolutely terrified. I started crying hysterically, and my uncle just laughed, as though my misery was amusing. These days, as much as the fear, I remember my resentment at him for not showing more sympathy."

"In fifth grade, I had to wear a special dental retainer that made it hard for me to speak clearly. Naturally, my classmates pointed out that I talked oddly and teased me. I was so devastated that for months I avoided speaking as much as possible. It never occurred to me then that *all* the kids got teased for something. Most of them rolled with it. Not me."

Sensitivity to Change

Ryan, whom we discussed at the beginning of this chapter, is sensitive to change and pace. He likes his novelty in small, manageable doses. Like many sensitive children, he suffers from a lack of fit between his temperament and the society at large.

What that society defines as "fun" for little kids—noise, kaleidoscopic sensations coming more-more-more, faster-faster-faster—can be extremely distressing to sensitive children. They are often miserable in just those settings in which people want and expect then to be delighted.

This is a live-for-the-moment culture. We are

urged to grab for all the gusto, to move into the fast lane. We are told that opportunity only knocks once, and he who hesitates is lost.

Yet he who hesitates may be a sensitive child who, by his very nature, needs to get his bearing in new situations. He needs to think things over and digest information before making a decision or taking action.

Children in this category often have what's described as negative initial reaction. That means that they genuinely dislike a new experience at the first exposure, although the same experience can please them when it becomes familiar.

The other trait that is common among these sensitive children is difficulty making the transition from one activity to another.

"My mother says I was impossible to take to the county fair because I always wanted to spend too long on each exhibit. I'd want to spend the whole day watching the chick-hatching exhibit, or just watching the man who filled up the helium balloons. I hated being torn away from something interesting. I felt that I'd barely started to mine the pleasures of the moment, before having to abandon it."

"When I was a child, I liked rainy days. That meant we didn't have to go out for recess. The other kids loved to burst outside into the fresh air, yelling and running around. That was always too chaotic for me, and I usually just stood on the sidelines until it was time to go in. But on rainy days, we could go to the cafeteria for quiet games, or even to the library to read. That was much less stressful for me."

ADULTS REFLECT ON SENSITIVITY

As we'll discuss in Chapter Nine, sensitive children often—but not always—become sensitive adolescents and adults. Although they may learn to improve their skills and cope quite nicely with their own temperament, they still have to manage in a world that does not always understand sensitivity.

"My roommate likes to have music while she studies. I can't even think clearly when there's loud music, much less concentrate on my work. The music and the words of the songs get all tangled up with what I'm reading, and I can't keep them sorted out. When I complain, she laughs and acts like I don't enjoy music or entertainment, which isn't true. I don't understand how she can work with music, and she doesn't understand why I can't."

"My son plays soccer, and the one thing I dread about the season is working in the snack bar at the field. It's always very hectic, with people crowding around ordering things, and me trying to find the ketchup for someone's hot dog and make change. Somehow it feels like I have to make one snap decision after another. And I have to make conversation with dozens of people, one after another. Other parents don't seem to mind this job as much as I do."

"In social situations, if I don't know *exactly* what to do or say, I freeze. It's not that I'm shy, exactly. I can really handle just about anything, as long as there's a script. I just need to know what to do, or I won't feel at ease. I can get up in front of a group and read a statement or a prepared speech—as long as I don't have to respond to questions afterward."

"My roommates used to complain that I was aloof and didn't like people because I would go into my room and close the door when people were over. But that wasn't true. I *do* like people, and I liked my roommates. I just used to get tired of interacting, and in need of being by myself. They couldn't understand that. I realize now that my reserve is probably temperamental. I am not a loner at all; I really need attachment and intimacy, but I get stressed after long periods of time with others, even people I like."

"In my work, I have to be able to approach people. It took me a while to get good at it, and even now I sometimes have to push myself, but I'm quite able to walk up to people and introduce myself. Most people would never guess that I'm shy."

THE COMFORT CONNECTION

As parents, we can better understand our sensitive children's feelings if we think of their temperament as a comfort zone, as a realm of equilibrium. Consider Emily, for example.

For the first few years of elementary school, her shyness kept her sidelined. She played by herself, worked by herself, never raised her hand. Finally, in second grade, something changed. Emily met another little girl, and they hit it off. They began working together, playing together, and boosting each other's confidence. "It was as though the personality she always had came out," said Emily's mother. "She didn't really change. She was just *comfortable*."

Meeting one other person is often a key to a shy child's ability to be comfortable in a group. But Emily's comfort zone was there all along. When she found another child with whom she could be comfortable and still be herself, she blossomed.

We all seek situations and experiences that are comfortable, and avoid those that are uncomfortable or stressful. And we vary in our perceptions of what's comfortable and what isn't; temperament, to a large degree, determines what behaviors and situations are comfortable.

Looking at our children's sensitivity from this

perspective helps us understand how persistent it is, and how difficult it is for a child to try different ways of behaving.

And yet, sensitive children need ways to manage in the real world, and that means parents need to help children expand the areas in which they feel comfortable. The key is to identify and enrich the child's zone of comfort. As children feel more at ease, they become less anxious, less hesitant, more ready to take the next step.

Just because something isn't in our nature, or isn't comfortable, doesn't mean we shouldn't have to do it, or learn techniques for getting ourselves to do it. Getting out of bed in the morning, going out and meeting people, picking up the phone to ask for a date, preparing for a job interview—all are experiences that may feel less than comfortable at the moment, but which need to be done if we are to live full lives.

As you strive to see the world through your sensitive child's eyes, you need to keep in mind this key point: Empathy is essential, but it is not enough. Your sensitive child needs to feel comfortable and cozy, some of the time. But she also needs to feel the exhilarating stress of being stretched, of striving to be just a little better, or stronger, than she was.

That means that your task is to structure her comfort so that instead of limiting her, it gives her strength and confidence. And you need to find and sometimes create opportunities for her to experience challenge and growth.

As she grows and becomes stronger and more capable, she will become—ultimately—more comfortable than her sensitive temperament might originally have permitted.

◆ 5 ◆

Parental Pitfalls:
Seventeen Well-Meaning Mistakes Parents
Make

Jared's parents have signed him up for two weeks of summer camp in the mountains. At age ten, Jared has never been away from home. He's spent the night at friends' houses a few times, but he doesn't like it. He finds it hard to sleep in an unfamiliar place. He worries about wetting the bed (even though he never does). He misses his parents.

His father has selected the camp he himself attended and loved as a child. Jared has made it clear that he doesn't want to go and insists that he'll hate it. His father says it's time for Jared to "grow up."

There is a possibility that Jared will "grow up" at camp and all will be well. But it's at least as likely that his camping experience will be miserable.

Obviously, you can't do much about your child's genetic blueprint, or his prenatal environment, or whether his temperament harmonizes with your own. However, as we outlined in Chapter One, the way you accept, manage, and direct your child's sensitivity—the interaction between temperament and life experience—is what sets your child's course for the future.

In the next chapter, we'll discuss the parental approaches that have the best track record in helping sensitive children develop and flourish. In this chapter, however, we'll examine some of the common errors that parents make.

Parenting sensitive children is challenging, as we've outlined in Chapter Three, because so often they do not respond to the very techniques that work well with most children. That's why it's so easy to get off course.

Ironically, it's the very love we have for our children that makes it so easy to act in ways that aren't always best for them. We may discipline harshly because we want so badly for them to be well-behaved, or set no limits at all because we want them to be happy. The parents most susceptible to making these errors tend to be the very ones who are the most devoted and conscientious.

Following are seventeen well-meaning mistakes that parents of sensitive children make:

Failure to Understand Sensitivity

Parents who sincerely believe that all children can be made to conform to certain behaviors may put too much pressure on their sensitive children. They may not recognize those aspects of behavior that are clearly related to temperament, and they may ascribe negative motives to their child.

In addition, parents who do not understand sensitivity may be unable to predict how their children will respond to certain settings and situations. For example, a fussy, colicky infant who screams at every change in his routine may be a child with a low sensory threshold. Until his parents understand that, they may keep trying to soothe the baby with lots of cuddling, bouncing, or extra bottles— providing *more* stimulation, when what he needs is less.

And it's much harder for parents to monitor the situations that cause difficulties for their children. They wander through the fairgrounds blissfully unaware that their sensitive child is gradually growing overwhelmed by the frantic music, the pushing crowds, the smells of people and popcorn and cotton candy. They may, then, be totally unprepared when their sensitive child becomes miserable and out of control.

Trying to Change Basic Temperament

"I hope he gets over his shyness by the time he starts school."

"This will make a man out of him!"

"You need to just roll up your sleeves and just *do* it!"

"She'll just have to learn to tune out those distractions and buckle down."

Statements like these suggest that sensitive children can somehow turn into different, more perfect human beings, and do so through an act of will. That's rarely possible. Certainly a sensitive child is capable of adapting to parental expectations in many ways, but he is unlikely to be able to change his *essential* temperamental bias. If he is shy and always has been, he will probably have a lifelong tendency toward shyness, although there is much he can do to increase his confidence and competence in social situations.

Jordan is an emotionally sensitive eight-year-old who is fearful of water. His father wants his son to get over his fear so he can enjoy the pleasures of swimming. One day at a family swim party, Jordan's father was so exasperated by his son's refusal to get wet that he scooped him up and waded with him into the shallow end. But Jordan screamed and scrambled out of the pool, spending the rest of the afternoon as far from the water as possible.

Most Jordans will eventually learn to swim, but their path will be smoother if their parents resist the temptation to "cure" them of their innate temperament.

Allowing Parents' Early Experiences to Define Expectations

"I was lonely and didn't make friends easily. I hope my daughter is going to be popular."

*   *   *

"One of the happiest memories from my childhood was when a huge gang of kids would get together and play 'Capture the Flag' on summer nights. We'd run around like crazy for hours, and it would get dark so gradually we didn't even realize it, until the fireflies came out. I want Greg to have as much fun as I did when I was his age."

"I grew up on a farm where there weren't many other children to play with. By the time I got to junior high school, the other kids had all been playing team sports for years. I would have loved to play, but I was too far behind. I'm going to make sure that Kevin doesn't miss his chance to play basketball or baseball."

In many ways, parents try to provide their children with what they themselves missed. If we grew up poor or didn't get an education, we struggle to give our children better opportunities. We also do this with emotional experiences as well, trying to protect our children from our own remembered hurts and supplying them with our remembered pleasures.

However, we are not our children. We can't undo our own childhood disappointments through them, nor can we relive our childhood pleasures in the same way. Our children will experience their own challenges and delights, not ours. A child who is socially sensitive may never be "popular" in the usual sense, but be perfectly content with a small circle of intimate friends. A child who hangs back from large group games, or who shows no interest in athletics, can have a happy childhood just the same.

Overprotecting

Ironically, parents who *do* understand and recognize their child's sensitivity can be at risk of trying to shelter him from all pain and distress.

Clara is intensely shy in situations where she must speak to strangers. She loves to read and asks her mother to get books from the library. Clara is now ten, but her mother still checks the books out on her own card rather than helping Clara learn to perform this simple task on her own.

Tyler is acutely sensitive to flavors, aromas, and food textures. As a toddler, he used to gag on his food and complain that it was too hard to chew. Now, at seven, his parents still cut his food for him. Tyler may still be more comfortable with his food cut in small pieces, but he's old enough to learn to cut it himself.

Overprotecting hinders the sensitive child's development in three ways:

- It reinforces the child's temperamental bias and does not allow him to take chances, to develop the skills he needs.

- It sends a negative message to a sensitive child. It says, "I guess I can't do this. I'm more comfortable not trying anyway, and Mom doesn't think I can handle it, so I guess I can't. And that's fine with me."
- Overprotective parents can get so caught up in their child's needs and all the subtle dimensions of his sensitivity that they genuinely come to believe that nobody else can possibly understand him. Who else could meet his needs, keep him functioning? It's easy to start running interference for a child, interpreting him to the world, the school, other adults, instead of helping him do some of this himself.

Overconsoling

Too much consoling and wiping away of tears can stand in the way of sensitive children's ability to move beyond their emotional tenderness. Certainly parental warmth and solicitousness are important, but they can be overdone.

Studies have suggested that when a mother of a sensitive, anxious infant cuddles and comforts her child very frequently—offering comfort even when it isn't sought—it may enhance the child's innate fearful tendencies as he grows up. A reasonable level of comfort, but not excess parental fussing, seems to help children manage their fears and anxieties later on.

Over time, parents of sensitive children can get

into a pattern of offering emotional comfort too quickly, even before it is needed or even asked for.

An emotionally sensitive seven-year-old rushes into the house and wails that her friend was "being mean." If her mother responds only by sharing the child's sorrow and offering hugs and sympathy, she may impair her daughter's ability to learn ways to get along with friends.

A better response might be to say, "I'd be upset too if someone called me a name. What can you say to Megan to solve this?"

Just as a toddler who is fed more than he wants may develop eating problems, a sensitive child who has sympathy urged on him may fail to develop confidence in his own ability to sense what he needs and when.

Using Language That Limits

The words that parents choose can affect their sensitive child's self-concept and also undermine her sense of competence.

"She's shy," announces a mother in the presence of her sensitive four-year-old. "She's even afraid to talk to Santa Claus!"

"You're such a worry wart," says another parent of her son.

"You're so *picky*. Who *cares* if your sandwich is cut in squares instead of triangles? Just eat it!"

"Don't be scared. It's nothing but a movie."

"Everybody else is enjoying the fireworks. Why are you crying? They're just noises. They won't hurt you."

"I don't care if you don't want to get out of the pool. You've got to stop being so stubborn. Just *do* it."

Negative language that labels a sensitive child has three effects:

- It demeans him. Words like *lazy, timid, crabby,* or *scatterbrained* may seem accurate to an outside observer. But sensitive children are not helped by hearing those labels.
- It deprives him of a sense that his feelings and inclinations are real and valid. Parents of sensitive children find themselves issuing emotional orders to their children. "Don't be afraid!" "Don't worry!" Although the message is positive, the bossy delivery can deny the child's valid feelings. Telling him not to be afraid, when he *is* afraid, creates a sense that he shouldn't feel what he really does feel.
- It gives him a sense of powerlessness. "I guess I am shy. I guess there's nothing I can do about it."

Parents of children who are sensitive (or have any other challenging temperamental trait) often find themselves asking lots of "why" questions of their children, such as: "Why don't you ever get ready when I call you?" or "Why can't you just eat what you're served and not complain about it?" or "Why do you always make such an issue about your clothes?"

These are rhetorical questions that really don't have an acceptable answer. (After all, what answer is really expected? "Well, since you asked, I guess I fuss about food because I have high levels of dopamine-beta-hydroxylase, which catalyzes the conversion of dopamine to norepinephrine in my brain, and so I'm sensitive to unfamiliar flavors.")

Failure to Prioritize

Parents of sensitive children are at risk of trying to correct too many imperfections simultaneously because they want to improve or "cure" their children of difficult behavior. Often, instead of focusing on the most important issues, they get bogged down in behaviors that aren't that important.

Like many sensitive children, James is particular about his clothing. He especially hates wearing shoes with laces and isn't able to explain to his mother exactly what it is that bothers him about them. On Sundays, she insists that he wear dress shoes with laces, rather than loafers which he prefers, and consequently, there's a major battle before church every week.

James's mother has made an ultimately small matter into a battleground. It isn't necessary for parents to win every battle or to make an issue out of every detail of their sensitive child's tastes and habits.

Spotlighting

When a sensitive child feels that all eyes are upon him—whether they're friendly eyes or glaring, critical ones—he feels that he is on stage, with all attention focused on him. Being in the spotlight is a sensation that magnifies sensitivity in anyone. After all, many adults, sensitive or otherwise, claim that their biggest fear is the thought of giving a speech before a large audience.

The sense of dread, the sweaty palms, the racing imagination that fast-forwards through all the possible disasters, all these sensations strike sensitive children when they feel they are being forced onto center stage. What makes them different from ordinary people with stage fright is that they perceive themselves to be spotlighted when well-meaning adults may not think they are doing that at all.

Elizabeth's parents were urging her to tell her neighbor what she got for Christmas. That didn't seem too much to ask. After all, it's polite to respond to another adult, even if you're a shy five-year-old. When Elizabeth balked, her parents pressed her. "Come on, Elizabeth! We're waiting! What did Santa bring you? Tell Mrs. Jones about your dollhouse!"

Another child would probably have announced his favorite toy, with a bit of gentle prodding. But to Elizabeth, the sensation of being under a microscope was too intense, and she froze.

Teasing

When eight-year-old Aaron's uncle visits, he always asks the kids about their girlfriends and boyfriends: "So, Aaron, who's your girlfriend this year?" None of the children actually has a sweetheart, of course, and the others just giggle and take the questions in stride. But Aaron cringes with embarrassment. He takes the question seriously: I don't have one. Am I supposed to? Why does he ask when he knows the answer? And why is everyone laughing at me?

Sensitive children often read more into casual situations than is really there. They may take things literally, not understand a joke, or have difficulty with ordinary teasing.

Certainly friendly, good-natured humor (like serving penguin and squid sauce for supper) is unlikely to cause damage to a sensitive child, although it may not be appreciated. But when teasing gets personal, veering too close to the child's quirks, habits, or inadequacies, it can be devastating.

If a sensitive child wears only certain clothes that feel comfortable to him, blushes when meeting new people, is frightened of the neighbor's dog or hates birthday parties, being teased about these behaviors will probably be more painful than it might be to less sensitive children.

Yelling

"What does *not* work is yelling," conceded one mother of an emotionally sensitive son. "Unfortunately, that's what I tend to do. I get so frustrated when he resists everything. I'm beginning to realize that he's not doing this to me to be nasty. He really is upset."

Shouting and yelling as a means of guiding our children is generally not effective. But with sensitive children, it's particularly ineffective. They may be stubborn, balky, resistent to following orders, but often the behavior is not under their control. And it's particularly distressing for children who are sensitive to noise.

But most of all, angry words from a parent can feel very much like a personal rejection to a sensitive child.

Clare, age six, refused to use a public restroom during a family trip because "it smells funny." Inevitably, then, as the family was back on the freeway, she announced in a small voice that she had to go.

Clare's father, already exasperated by traffic, lost

his temper and screamed. Clare already felt unsettled being away from home and being expected to tolerate uncomfortable experiences. Having her father sound so angry, on top of everything else, felt like the end of the world.

Explaining too Much

As you'll see in Chapter Six, providing a lot of background information and preparing a sensitive child for new situations is an excellent tool, in particular for children who are emotionally sensitive and for children who have trouble being comfortable in unfamiliar situations.

However, some parents, go overboard in their efforts to ease the child's way. They go over every detail, every possibility, and their anxiety can be conveyed to the child, making his comfort level even lower.

"We'll leave early in the morning, because it's the first day of camp, and we want you to be on time. We'll pack your backpack the night before so you won't forget anything, and you'll be sure to have your snack money and your water bottle. We'll register you at the gym and hand in all the forms we filled out and the medical form explaining what to do if you get stung by a bee. Then you'll put on your name tag and meet your counselor, and then we'll say good-bye and you'll have a great time until four when I pick you up."

Swashbuckling

Especially if you are not sensitive (or not sensitive in the same way your child is), be wary of prattling on about your bold, daring, and dramatically nonsensitive childhood. "When I was a kid we used to camp outside. No tents! Every morning before breakfast we'd run down to the freezing lake and jump right in!"

Parents often are eager to inspire their sensitive child to try new things by telling about their own enjoyable experiences. But when the stories are about events or activities that the child finds scary or not to his liking, they can increase the pressure he feels and add to his sense of hopelessness about measuring up.

Naturally you'll want to share your childhood experiences with your child. But do this sharing tactfully. If you were captain of the football or cheerleading team, if you were voted class president or most popular, these revelations—if repeated endlessly—may make your socially sensitive child feel like a failure.

Failure to Discipline

Sensitive children are often more compliant and better-behaved than most children, so for many parents, discipline is less of a concern. But not all sensitive children are easygoing. They can lose control, throw tantrums, and manipulate with the best of them.

That's especially true when the sensitive child has learned to use his own temperament as a tool. Because he gets so upset so dramatically, a sensitive child can easily train his parents to tiptoe around his temperament, rather than help him modify it.

Lauren, age nine, is emotionally sensitive. When she is upset or feels that she has been wrongly criticized, she becomes distraught and cries. So when Lauren's parents ask her to share with her brother, do a chore, or tidy up a mess she has made, they brace themselves for the signs of a meltdown: the woeful face, the soft whimpers. Often, they decide it's easier for all concerned to let her off easy.

"Jason won't go to bed until he's sleepy. And he doesn't get sleepy until about nine o'clock. When we tried to make him go to bed earlier, he threw a tantrum."

Lauren may be emotionally sensitive, and Jason may have trouble with transitions and schedule changes. But they need firm, loving discipline, just as all children do.

Burdening a Sensitive Child With Adult Concerns

Sensitive children, especially those who are emotionally sensitive and perceptive, may seem more mature than they really are. It can be tempting for some parents to treat such children as miniature adults.

Katrina, age ten, is remarkably sensitive to the needs and feelings of others. Her parents are divorced, and she lives with her mother. Katrina picks up on the tensions her mother experiences in her efforts to earn a living, be a single parent, and develop a social life of her own. She asks her mother about her day, listens well, and makes perceptive comments and suggestions; the relationship between the two is more like girlfriends than mother and daughter.

Certainly, Katrina's emotional sensitivity and perceptiveness are strengths that will serve her well throughout her life. But she is temperamentally susceptible to anxieties and may become excessively anxious, unless Katrina's mother is able to shield her daughter from full-strength adult worries and concerns.

Assigning Motives

Sensitive children can be stubborn and exasperating. It's easy for parents to fall into the trap of assigning motives to their children that aren't necessarily present. This is particularly true when parent and child have different temperaments. The parent is mystified by what motivates the child and says, "She's doing this just to drive me crazy!"

Assigning motives contributes to a victim mentality in parents and puts the child in the driver's seat, rather than helping the parents muster the authority and confidence they need. And it can make the sensitive child feel wronged and misunderstood by the parent.

Forgetting That They Grow Up

Often the parents of sensitive children do an excellent job at a certain age or stage but forget to reevaluate what works and what doesn't as their child matures.

What you expect of your child needs to be expanded as his abilities and skills develop. Maybe a few years ago he simply was incapable of picking up the phone and calling another child for a playdate, and you handled that task so at least he had play opportunities. But now he's in fourth grade and needs to take steps to take over that function for himself.

You might order for your shy fifth grader in restaurants now. But unless you work out ways to hand the reins over to her, you'll be running interference with the waitress when your child is thirty.

You might be careful to arrange quiet, calm birthday parties for your sensitive-to-change five-year-old. But as she grows more mature, her ability to handle noise and excitement should increase. If you automatically stick to the old ways, you may miss the fact that by her eleventh birthday, she feels ready to try a slumber party with a large group of friends.

Perfectionism

If your child is sensitive, he will always be challenging to some degree. There is no way to convert him into an entirely different child. Your life together may always involve some compromises, some give-and-take.

And if your child isn't perfect, neither are you. You will probably never get the Perfect Parent of the Year award. You will do better at some aspects of your parenting job, and less well at others. Dwelling only on the failures blinds you to all the successes, big and small, that your child has achieved.

Many of the mistakes parents make with their sensitive children are the natural outgrowth of their desire to help and encourage.

A sensitive, shy, anxious child obviously needs more friends, and so the temptation of the parent who desperately wants to make the child happy is to produce a crowd of playmates. Yet that approach not only fails to allow the child to learn, at his own pace, the art of friendship; it also runs the risk of frightening or overwhelming a socially sensitive child.

Often a head-on approach to solving temperament problems isn't the best way. The most effective approach is often indirect, and almost counterintuitive, the way you see a faint star more clearly by looking at it indirectly.

In the following chapter, we outline those techniques for working with—not against—your child's sensitivity and helping him grow.

◆ 6 ◆

Techniques That Work:
What Really Helps Your Sensitive Child Thrive and Grow

If you were to watch twelve-year-old Adam at the beach on a hot July day, you would not consider him a sensitive child. You would watch him kick off his flip-flops, race across the sand, and hurtle into the surf like a porpoise.

Yet six years ago, Adam's sensitivity was painfully obvious. He hated adjusting to the cold water. He was afraid of sinking, and he worried about his inability to swim. So for most of that summer, he stayed on dry land. At a friend's swimming pool, he would cling to the side and refuse to release his grip—even in the shallow end.

How did Adam progress from his cramped, timid style to his glorious day at the beach?

He did it by growing up, as all children do, and he did it with the wise assistance of his parents, who understood the basics of helping a sensitive child blossom.

MANAGING SENSITIVITY: THE BASICS

Loving and nurturing a sensitive child requires striking a balance between two fundamental needs:

First, your child needs to be loved as she is, sensitivity and all. And that love and acceptance needs to come from you, and from within herself.

Second, she needs to acquire skills and experiences that will help her flourish, even if acquiring those skills and experiences does not come naturally to her.

If the first requirement is neglected—lots of practice with skills, but little positive acceptance—the sensitive child runs the risk of sinking deeper into her sense of powerlessness and failure. If the second requirement is neglected and she gets too much coddling and not enough challenge, she runs the risk of languishing in a comfort zone that will not prepare her for adult life.

It is one hallmark of sensitive children that they often do not push themselves into situations that other children welcome. Other children jump into the swimming pool; you have to worry that they'll go in over their heads. Your sensitive child shivers on the side of the pool; you worry that she'll never take the plunge.

Your task is to find that balance between giving her the time she needs to take on new challenges, and making sure that she has challenges to meet.

As your child grows, she will take over more and

more of this role. Your role will gradually evolve from hands-on manager to that of mentor and consultant.

Following are some basic suggestions that apply to a range of sensitive children:

Teach Her About Sensitivity

As you talk about sensitivity with your child, you've been giving her the language to understand her temperament. As she grows older, you can help her learn more about temperament and how it works.

You can explain what you've learned about the biological basis for certain aspects of sensitivity, and that people are born with different patterns of brain structure. You can remind your child that being particularly alert, quick to sense danger, or cautious about unfamiliar situations are all valuable traits that have helped individuals and groups survive.

Whether your own temperament is similar to your child's or quite different, you can discuss it with her. "I know you like to come home and go up to your room by yourself," you might say. "You find it restful to be alone for a while. I get restless when I have to spend a lot of time with no one to talk to. That's one of the ways we're different."

As your sensitive child grows, she will learn that the outside world may neither understand nor celebrate sensitivity as much as her family does. She will need to internalize positive messages and be capable of explaining temperament to others.

Give Her Time

Sensitive children do not become bold and assertive overnight. But they can progress if their progress is measured in digestible quantities.

Adam's progress from a reluctant swimmer to an enthusiastic surfer took years of patience and encouragement. As Adam's body and his confidence grew, every small success laid the foundations for another success.

Every other child in your neighborhood may already be comfortable staying home alone, but your own eleven-year-old gets upset and anxious. Yes, she'll need to learn some independence, but you can work on it gradually. She doesn't have to do it right now, this year, if it's difficult for her.

However, although you may present new demands and experiences gradually, and according to your child's individual rate of development, that doesn't mean you won't make some demands and offer opportunities.

Sometimes parents know their sensitive child too well—they simply *know* he won't want to go to the beach, or to the pizza restaurant—so they save everybody the aggravation by not going at all.

But even sensitive children do grow up, and the experience that overwhelmed your child last year may be manageable this year. If your child dreaded the idea of day camp last summer, don't rule it out. Consider it again this summer, or next.

Prioritize

With all children, it's important to have a sense of proportion. There are some issues of discipline, schedule, safety, and courtesy that are nonnegotiable. Your child has to go to school, may not play in the street, and must not hurt the baby.

Other issues just aren't as important: whether a child has syrup or powdered sugar on her waffles; whether she wears jeans or sweatpants out to play; whether she sits on Santa's lap.

With sensitive children, the importance of prioritizing is more than important. It's essential, because sensitive children have to work harder at developmental tasks. They can't afford to squander their energies on minor issues.

"Where is it written that you have to go to every birthday party, just because you're invited?" asks one mother of a sensitive seven-year-old. Where, indeed? And where is it written that your daughter has to try out for the talent show, even if she's frightened of performing before a group?

In fact, says this mother, "You have to think, 'What's really important for him to do? What can I give up on?' "

With sensitive children, your task is to reduce battles over trivial items and save your heavy fire for the things that really matter. Does your child *have* to learn to ride a horse? Attend the sixth grade dance?

You'll have plenty to do on those issues that really are important. For example, your sensitive child really does need to get an education. Your preschooler may have to be in day care. She has to face some of her fears, like going to the doctor. She has to be away from you some of the time, even if she doesn't like it.

These are the must-dos, and you and your child should concentrate on these.

Others, like Santa's lap and the issue about what clothes to wear, can be eliminated from the agenda.

Finally, others are negotiable. You'd like your child to attend soccer camp so she'll have some daytime activity during the summer, but if she's strongly opposed, you may choose not to press it. Or, you and she might work out a deal. She doesn't have to attend the party, if she would rather not, but she has to make her own apologies to the host.

Just as you set priorities when your child is small, your older sensitive child will need to take over this task by making her own choices. More and more, the task of deciding which issues are important and which are not will fall to her.

Break Things Down

Maybe your shy daughter can't tell the waitress what she wants, but she can learn to say "thank you" when the server brings the food.

If you try to get your sensitive child to make a major life change all at once, the task can seem overwhelming and she'll probably shrink from it. If, on the other hand, you can break challenges down into small parts that she is more likely to master, she'll be more willing to try and experience more success.

Once a difficult task is broken down, it becomes easier for your child to build on her progress. Perhaps she'd love to be in school theater productions, but the idea of trying out and performing in public feels overwhelming. Maybe this year she could help paint scenery, set up chairs, or hand out programs. The social experience and confidence she gains from succeeding at small tasks makes the more challenging tasks seem possible.

Emphasize Progress

Point out to your sensitive child that she can do things now that she couldn't do a few years ago. "I remember when you played in the shallow end the whole time. Now you're jumping into eight feet of water!"

But take care not to gush about every positive behavior. Sensitive children, more than others, pick up on the kind of exaggerated praise that parents use when they lack confidence in their child.

When the parent says, "There, see? You asked that child to play. Now you've made a friend. Gooooood for you!!!" the child senses the the praise is forced and ultimately insincere. A sensitive child, then, may interpret the comment to mean, "Whew! What a relief! I was afraid you'd *never* find someone to play with."

Watch Your Language

How you define your child's sensitivity to her is important. So, too, is how she expresses her own discomfort. Even very young children benefit from knowing and using the right terms for feelings. If your three-year-old is fussy about clothing, you can help her acquire the language necessary to explain her feelings.

The key to defining your child's sensitivity in an affirming, positive way, is to use positive words for the most basic, unchanging aspects of temperament. Those are qualities that make her herself, that make her special. You might say, "You're the only person in this family who can taste the little bit of curry I added. You have a very keen sense of smell."

You needn't sugarcoat a particular behavior that your child needs to change. If your child has a tantrum because the bakery put green icing on her birthday cake, instead of the orange icing she expected, there's no point in saying positive things about the tantrum.

However, after you've dealt with the inappropriate behavior, you might say, "I know you don't like surprises. You feel better when everything is just what you expect."

Your child can learn to control her outbursts, or other inappropriate behavior, with your help. But she probably will never change her discomfort with novelty, or her strong desire to have everything just the same. She'll still feel like a worthwhile person if you can define that desire in positive terms, all the while helping her temper her reactions.

For example:

- Instead of "You're so picky!" you can say, "You notice things other people don't," or "You're very particular and selective about how things feel."
- Instead of saying, "You're scared of your own shadow," you can say, "You're careful," or "You like to make sure you'll be safe before you climb anything."
- Instead of "You're shy," you can say, "You're cautious about meeting new people."
- Instead of "You're a loner," you can say, "You feel more comfortable when you have some time to think your own thoughts without being distracted."

You'll notice that the negative phrases bring the discussion to a halt. All they do is label and express disapproval.

But the positive phrases open the door to constructive suggestions and helpful discussions, such as, "You like to make sure things are safe before you go ahead. How can we find out if this dog is friendly?" Or, "We have to do your back-to-school shopping this weekend. I know you don't enjoy rushing from one thing to another. We'll probably have a busy schedule. Any thoughts on how we can make it easier for you?"

Language also helps your sensitive child understand her own temperament and make her needs known. From the time she can say or understand the concept of "too much," she can use words to explain what's upsetting her. She can say, "too hot," "too loud," or "too scratchy." Later, she can say, "it's stinky," or "it pinches right there."

Naturally, there will be times—especially with younger sensitive children—when the response is a flat, "No! I hate that!" You can respond with respect, saying, "Can you tell me what bothers you about this jacket? (or sandwich, or whatever). If you explain it to me, I'll be able to pick out something better next time."

Eventually, your child's ability to explain her temperament and her behavior to others will help her manage on her own. She'll be able to say, "I'll wait outside. All the noise and activity makes me uncomfortable."

Focus on behavior, not emotions

Your child has a right to feel what she feels, but she is responsible for what she chooses to do about those feelings. She may feel sad, upset, or anxious, but she doesn't have to dissolve in tears or have a tantrum.

Nine-year-old Cassie has two friends visiting. The three girls are having an animated discussion in Cassie's room. Someone's feelings get hurt. The door bursts open and Cassie rushes out in tears. "Nicole and Molly weren't being nice to me," she cries. Her mother says, "That may be, but crying is not the answer. You'll have to wipe your eyes and go back and find another way. Let me know how it works out."

Provide a buffer

As we discussed in Chapter Five, it's tempting to overprotect sensitive children. And while that temptation must be resisted, that doesn't mean that parents shouldn't be protective at all.

While it's essential that you encourage your sensitive child to go out and try new experiences, you don't need to send her out without any survival gear. Your task is to provide your child with a sort of space suit that allows her to venture into seemingly hostile environments and be able to explore freely.

This is true for all children, whether they're sensitive or not. Like a two-year-old with a pacifier or a favorite teddy bear, a child who feels protected and prepared will accept challenges more readily than one who feels vulnerable.

But the development of buffers is particularly important for sensitive children, who often feel intensely vulnerable. They might be something as plain and simple as a pair of soft, comfortable socks to ease the pinchy shoes, or earplugs that allow a child to feel comfortable going to the fireworks display.

Or they can be emotional, like a pep talk or a hug from a parent. One father sings, "Don't Worry, Be Happy" to his emotionally sensitive son in stressful situations.

And buffers can be social, as when you encourage your child to bring a close friend to a gathering at which she might feel shy and isolated. Whether they're physical objects or internalized attitudes, buffers boost confidence and allow the child to extend her range.

Over time, your child will need to take the responsibility for knowing what sort of buffering she needs and then taking care of it herself.

If she has trouble with clothing, she can learn to shop for herself, take responsibility for her choices, and adjust her clothing so it's comfortable. She can make her own decisions about what kind of entertainment will upset her or what kind of social events she can cope with.

Give a demonstration

If you and your child are both sensitive in the same way, you may be able to convey ways to cope almost effortlessly. She may pick up the way you handle too much stress, too many people, or difficult transitions just by watching you.

But you'll probably need to clue your child in about what you're doing. For example, you might say, "I get upset when there's too much noise. It's hard for me to concentrate with all those children making so much noise. So what I usually do is bring a book and sit over on this bench."

You can convey information and techniques to your child at the same time that you are sending a supportive message.

As we described in Chapter Four, you can understand your child's temperament, even if you do not share it. So even if your own temperament is not sensitive, you can demonstrate techniques for managing and talk about them as you're doing them.

Remind her that things get easier

If you've ever applied for a mortgage, started a new job, changed a tire, or prepared your own taxes, you know that tasks that seem overwhelming the first time you do them seem easier the second and third times. This is especially true for sensitive children, who often experience more than the normal amount of stress when tackling a new task.

If your sensitive child is old enough to understand, convey to her that adults, too, deal with unfamiliarity and anxiety all the time—and manage to cope.

"I remember how hard it was to meet people my first day of camp. I didn't know anybody, and I couldn't figure out where anything was. All I could manage the first day was to find my bunk and say 'Hi' a few times.

"But the second day, it all seemed more familiar, and by the third day, it felt like home!"

As your child progresses, your reminders can include references to her own accomplishments. "Remember how hard it was to figure out these streets when we came here last summer? You seem to know your way around like a native now."

Use confidence-boosting tricks of the trade

Your sensitive child needs to know that most adults—not just the sensitive ones—need a boost sometimes to build their own confidence and keep their comfort level high in challenging situations.

There's a song from *The King and I* that builds courage with a reminder that acting brave is almost as good as the real thing. By whistling a happy tune, you realize that "You may be as brave as you make believe you are."

Public speakers use a favorite trick when their audience is particularly powerful, unsympathetic, or otherwise intimidating: They visualize every last one of them sitting there in their underwear. Somehow it puts everything in perspective.

What these tricks do is prevent unfamiliar people from assuming godlike proportions. And that's the essential point. Your child may feel uneasy, worried about saying the wrong things. But other people have weaknesses and worries too, whether they're theatergoers in the audience, coworkers at a meeting, or fellow guests at a social gathering.

Hold a dress rehearsal

Role-playing and rehearsing are effective tools for easing a sensitive child's discomfort about an upcoming event.

Role-playing can be a simple game: "I'll be Mrs. Hillman, and you can be you. Let's pretend that I come up and say, 'Hello, Meredith. How was your vacation?'"

Then Meredith practices looking Mrs. Hillman in the eye and saying, "Fine, thank you."

If your preschooler has trouble with transitions, you can make a teddy bear or puppet take on her role. "Teddy doesn't like to stop playing and get ready for bed. Let's see if we can teach him what he does first. When he's all ready, how many stories will we read him?" The key is to put your child into the role of teacher or mentor, so that she gets experience talking a sensitive teddy bear through a difficult situation.

Rehearsing is an effective way of providing a sensitive child with a skill that she can then use herself.

Michael, who is eleven, is a shy child who has trouble with spontaneous conversations. He is especially uncomfortable with compliments, because he feels he ought to say something that measures up to the compliment. After all, here is someone saying he's wonderful, and he can't think of anything wonderful to say.

One day, after Michael won an academic award, he confided to his father, "I wish I could just say 'thank you' and leave it at that."

"And why not?" replied his father. "That's all you really need to say. I think that's a good idea."

"Thank you!" said Adam, and they both laughed.

After some practice, Adam's "thank-yous" popped right out, accompanied by a broad smile. They seemed natural and spontaneous, because he had practiced them until they became second nature.

Make a plan

Older children, especially, benefit greatly from setting goals and making plans for dealing with sensitivity issues. A child who dreams of running for class president can learn to break big tasks down into smaller ones. She might set intermediate goals, like joining an organization so she can meet more people. Later, she might volunteer to help out at a dance or car wash. Whether or not she ever reaches the point that she gets elected to office, she will have made more progress by setting reasonable goals than unreasonable ones.

Even when the sensitive child is entirely realistic, long-term goals can seem overwhelming.

Leah, who is twelve, is socially sensitive, emotionally sensitive, and sensitive to change. She is academically talented and has an Ivy League college in mind. Yet she wonders, "How will I ever go away to college if I can't even bear to be away from home for one night?"

So Leah and her father work out an agenda with a series of intermediate goals that are reasonably attainable. This summer, she's going to concentrate on inviting one close friend to sleep at her house. Then, she'll try sleeping at the friend's house. If she can manage, she'll try sleep-overs with other close friends.

Next summer, she'll spend a weekend with her aunt and uncle. If that works, she'll attend a weekend retreat sponsored by her church.

The following summer, if she feels ready, she'll try two weeks of away-from-home summer camp. If she doesn't feel ready, she'll repeat the previous summer's activities for another year.

Leah developed her plan with her father's help

and support, but it is *Leah's* plan, not his. Leah is moving toward her own goals at a pace that stretches her, yet still feels comfortable.

Encourage, don't push

Finding that distinction between encouraging and pushing is an art. It's a bit different for every parent-child unit. As a parent, you do want to encourage your sensitive child to stretch just a bit— but always in ways that seem possible to your child.

Encouragement generally feels good to a child. You feel like her advocate and friend. And encouragement moves her in the direction she wants to go, and toward a goal she thinks she might be able to reach. Pushing pressures a child to be something she feels she has no hope of being, or pushes her toward something she wouldn't want even if he could.

If you tell your shy eleven-year-old daughter, "I signed you up for modeling classes! You'll just love it!" that feels like pressure. A better approach might be, "I just heard that Jennifer's mom is going to teach a modeling class down at the Community Center. Since you're going to take at least one class this summer, you might want to think about that one, too."

Following are some techniques for helping your child manage according to her fundamental style of sensitivity.

LOW SENSORY THRESHOLD

How to help: Encourage your sensitive child's input

From infancy on, your sensitive child needs to be handled with a gentler touch than other children. You'll need to be aware of temperature, noise levels, milk and bath temperature, even if you and your other children never noticed these issues.

But as she grows, you'll need to encourage her participation in managing her own comfort. The more input she has into decisions that affect her, the more easily she will be able to take over this management task herself.

When your child is very young, you'll do much of this management yourself. As your child grows, you'll need to introduce new things gradually, especially new foods. If you understand your child's low sensory threshold, you'll be able to handle refusal and rejection more calmly and philosophically. If your child spits out pureed carrots this week, you can back off and try again next week, or the week after that.

As your child begins dressing herself, she'll need the chance to make choices about clothing. If she will wear only sweatpants and no jeans or trousers, then buy sweatpants during these fussy years. If she complains about scratchy tags or lining, remove or cover them.

If you sympathize with your child's sensitive "pinchy" toes and let her make choices about her footwear, she will be able to make herself comfortable and move beyond her sensitivity more easily than she would if you forced her to be uncomfortable.

That's the approach Eric's parents took. You may remember that they were avid campers, and Eric tended to fuss and hold back because he was physically sensitive.

"We realized that what made us like camping so much wasn't sore feet and mosquito bites," his father said. "The real fun is being out in the beautiful natural setting, hiking in the clean air."

So they worked with Eric to find ways to buffer his sensitivity. He wore his old, comfortable sneakers, instead of official hiking boots. He got doused in bug spray. His parents agreed to choose easier hiking trails when Eric was along, and let him choose whether he wanted to go along on some of the tougher climbs.

Instead of complaining about Eric's shortcomings, they said things like, "Last time the bugs bothered you. What can we do to make you more comfy this time?"

Eric, for his part, agreed to go on some of the hikes and to cut back on his complaining.

As he grows older, Eric will be able to handle more of this process on his own. And as he takes more control of his comfort issues, he'll be less likely to complain to others.

It's helpful to remind sensitive children that

they're going to be all right, even if something is bothering them. If your child is fussing about lunch, you can say, "The sandwich is just fine, even though it's cut in half instead of in triangles the way you like it." Or, "The sand in your bathing suit feels scratchy, but it will rinse off easily. Then the scratchy feeling will be gone."

These statements help validate your child's feelings and preferences, and signal that it's okay to dislike the way a sandy bathing suit feels. Over time, these comments will convey the idea that these little problems aren't life-threatening, and that they can be managed. Yet it's often these very words that never get spoken, because parents become impatient and exasperated with the child's behavior.

As your child gets a bit older, she can learn to place some limits on complaining behavior, especially when she is away from the family. You can tell your child that complaining a lot has an effect on other people, so she'll need to manage her own discomforts in a way that doesn't necessarily call attention to them.

SOCIAL SENSITIVITY

How to help: Lots of relaxed practice

Social sensitivity, as we've discussed, comes in two forms: traditional shyness, which involves a sense of distress and anxiety, and solitary behavior, which is generally a choice.

Both kinds, however, require some modification because they can lead to isolation and lost opportunities to develop social skills. So your sensitive child does need opportunities to meet and play with others. And whether your child is classically shy or just self-sufficient, she will need the chance to practice those skills in relaxed, low-risk settings. (For more suggestions for helping traditionally shy children, see Chapter Seven.)

Some suggestions:

- Focus on quality of friendships, not quantity. Shy or quiet children often do not need many friends to be happy or to practice their social interactions. A few close friends will do just as well.
- Teach "approaching" skills if your child wants to interact, but is afraid to approach. Again, language helps here. You can have your preschooler practice phrases like, "Can I play?" and "What are you doing?" Older children can learn practice skills like making eye contact, and saying, "Hi, I'm Jordan. What's your name?" These approaches aren't easy for shy children, but they're more likely to use them if they've practiced.
- If your child is shy with strangers but fairly comfortable with someone she knows well, have her approach a group by focusing on one child. At a picnic, you might say, "There's a boy about your age playing with the Frisbee. Let's see if he'd like someone to throw it back to him."

"As soon as Amanda finds someone to relate to, one-to-one, she's fine," said the mother of a shy five-year-old. "Then, she's part of a team, and she's not afraid to take part. She doesn't feel so self-conscious. It's as if that other child acts as a shield."

- Remember that a child who is socially sensitive needs positive attention and experiences that build self-esteem just as much as the little ham who leaps on stage and performs at the drop of a hat. All children need to be noticed in positive ways. It's easy to overlook this need in shy children because they seem to avoid all sorts of attention, positive or otherwise.

- Rehearse social interactions. Anna is shy and finds it difficult to say anything at all with people she doesn't know well. Now, at twelve, she is applying to a private school that requires an entrance interview before acceptance.

As the interview date approached, Anna and her parents set up mock interviews at home. One of her parents would be the interviewer and ask questions of the kind likely to be asked in the real interview.

"What this did was give Anna time to think about her answers," said her mother. "She's the kind of child who finds it impossible to answer unless she's sure she has the right answer. This kind of practice gets her thinking ahead of time about what to say, and she goes into the real situation with more confidence."

Some socially sensitive children are not afraid

of social interaction, but rather are stressed by it. They may enjoy playing with other kids, but after a period of play, they need to decompress and do this by seeking solitude.

- Let your shy child know that just about everybody feels shy some of the time. Many adults feel a bit anxious walking into a room full of strangers. So there's nothing weird about feeling nervous and sweaty-palmed.

- Do provide your sensitive child with a place to be by herself, and time to retreat into solitude. If she doesn't have her own room, designate a space (a porch, a basement game room) somewhere else that's her "recharging" area if she needs to get away.

- Go over etiquette skills. Often, socially sensitive children withdraw from social situations because they are afraid of making an error, or not knowing how to respond to some unanticipated situation. They can appear rude. Practice is the best remedy. To the extent that your sensitive child knows how to greet people, to thank them, to make introductions, and to make courteous requests, she will be much more at ease.

EMOTIONAL SENSITIVITY

How to help: Ease hurt with fantasy play and reality testing

Like children with low sensory threshold, emotionally sensitive children need a way of shielding themselves from what bothers them. But shielding and buffering don't go far enough. A child with low sensory threshold can probably cope fairly well by figuring out ways to reduce physical irritations in her life. But it's a lot easier to find comfortable underwear than it is to conquer fears or avoid all scary situations. So emotionally sensitive children must learn to manage and "de-fang" some of their fears and anxieties.

Very young emotionally sensitive children need the most buffering, so it's best to eliminate anxiety-producing situations as much as possible. Just as you might put pads in your child's shoes, you can work to eliminate scary or stressful situations.

Some suggestions:

• Buffer your anxious child against stressful entertainment. Movies and television are more intense than they were when today's adults were children. Watching violent ninjas, criminals, and "Terminators" on screen can contribute to nightmares and worries.

• Buffer your sensitive child by providing an imaginary amulet she can take with her into stressful situations. It might be no more than a phrase: She might whisper to herself, "I can give this book report because I practiced and I know what to say."

• If you, also, have an emotionally sensitive temperament, try to minimize your own fears and anxieties. If you shudder at the sight of a snake, or stew about burglars and tornadoes and kidnappers and terrorists, your anxieties will be contagious. You don't need to deny them, but don't display your phobias in full 3-D glory.

- Respect your child's fear. Don't tell your frightened child, "Don't be scared." If she's scared, she's scared.
- Reassure, but reassure briefly and calmly. Don't elaborate endlessly on your child's fears—in a sense, giving them more legitimacy than they deserve. At the time your child is fearful, be calm and supportive, then move on. There will be other times you can discuss the specifics of the fear, and her own temperament, when she's not particularly scared.
- Rehearse situations that have your child worried (but don't go into such detail that the child's tension is heightened). A child who feels anxious before camp can practice packing his camp bag, looking over the map, and reciting the name of his counselor.
- Encourage reasonable risk-taking. Emotionally sensitive children can get boxed in by their worries, and unless they learn to take some well-chosen risks, they will limit their options in life.

For example, you might suggest that your child try something new at a restaurant. You could go over all possible outcomes of her choice. First, she might like the new food, and the result would be that she would enjoy it. Or, she might not like the food, and then she would be allowed to order something else. When your child does take a plunge, you can praise her for the progress she has made.

- If your child is unusually precise, obsessive, compulsive, or perfectionist, make a game of "messing up." Make a tower of blocks and knock it over with a joyous "Ooops!" Draw a picture full of incongruities, like the horse in the water and the fish flying in the air, to convey that it's possible to have fun with things not being quite right. Your child may protest, but sneak these games in when possible and she may join in. Generally, humor helps in these games, as long as the joke is not on your child.

- Use fantasy to help your child experience being confident and in control. Let your child act out being big and brave: king, queen, boss, train engineer, teacher, Mom, huge hungry monster.

- The child whose feelings are easily hurt, who complains that "everybody hates me," may need your help in learning to survive ordinary childhood teasing (and to distinguish between trivial kidding and behavior that's *really* mean).

The key is to chart a course that respects your child's feelings, on one hand, and avoids over-consoling, on the other.

If your daughter comes home from school crying because "everybody was mean to me," you can validate her feelings by saying, "Wow, you do seem pretty sad. What happened?" That's a much more effective opener than "Oh, don't be silly. Your friends wouldn't be mean to you."

After your daughter explains what happened,

you can determine whether she was truly the victim of bullying, or whether she is overreacting, as emotionally sensitive children often do. Then you can get her thinking about solutions:

"Sometimes other kids say things without realizing how much they hurt. Does Lauren say things like that to Sarah? What does Sarah do?"

"Can you think of another way to let her know you don't like it, other than crying?"

"How might you tell Lauren that you don't like her to call you names? Could you find a way that doesn't hurt *her* feelings?"

Teach some of the "antiteasing" behaviors that come more naturally to more confident children: ignoring, laughing, walking away, or defusing with a comment ("Yeah, *right*," or "Give me a break!").

- Turn the typical "what-if?" query of the anxious child into a constructive exercise. Instead of saying, "Oh, that won't happen" when your child worries about getting lost, you might say, "What if you *did* get lost? What are some things you could do?"

  Clearly, if this kind of exchange seems to distress your sensitive child, you would want to ease up. But for most children, thinking through the "what-ifs" and identifying some specific actions they could take actually decreases anxiety.

- Similarly, if your child is oversensitive to teasing, you might try a role-playing in which she practices teasing you, or you tease her and she practices ignoring or laughing off the teasing.

SENSITIVITY TO CHANGE

How to help: Don't take "no" for an answer

"One summer I enrolled Eric in a week of soccer camp, a week of baseball camp, a week here and a week there—I thought I'd be doing him a favor," said the mother of a nine-year-old who is sensitive to change. "He loves sports, and I wanted him to have a chance to try different activities so he wouldn't get bored. What a mistake! Every Monday was a nightmare as he agonized about getting to know new people, figuring out a new place. What I should have done is enroll him in one camp for the whole summer. Then he would go through this anguish once and be done with it!"

With the best of intentions, Eric's mother went too far in the direction of encouraging her sensitive son to try new things.

Other parents might go too far in the other direction: "Let's not upset him by asking him if he wants to go to camp this year."

The key to encouraging this kind of sensitive child is to continue to offer new experiences, but to do so in small, tactful doses.

Sensitive children who tend to have a negative first reaction run the risk of missing out on enjoyable experiences because they can't bring themselves to grasp an opportunity when it's offered. It's just too new, too sudden, for them to feel comfortable accepting. So just as you might offer carrots to a sensitive infant several times before she takes a taste, you should offer your sensitive child the chance to try a new experience more than once.

Suppose you're at the science museum, and there's a huge walk-through model of the human heart. You think your child might be interested in going through, the way hundreds of other eager children are doing. But she says no, shaking her head firmly.

Don't be too quick to accept first refusal as her final offer. You can pave the way by saying:

"Okay, Lauren. Let's find something else to try over here. We can look at the dinosaur section, if you'd like. Then if you'd like to come back to the heart later, that's fine, too."

You'll have to find the right middle course between nagging Lauren ("Are you *sure* you don't want to see the model heart? Sure?") and letting her off the New Experience hook too easily.

Other suggestions:

- Do minimize the amount of change your child has to cope with. Buffer her against extreme demands, like starting a new camp, every week.
- Buffer your child against excess stimulation if that upsets her. Avoid, or cut short, visits to settings like malls and hectic entertainment centers.
- Allow your sensitive child to change her mind without losing face. If she initially refused an ex-

perience and then expresses an interest after all, don't criticize her for her inability to make up her mind.

As your child gets older, she will learn to give herself second chances. A child whose first reaction to something new is usually negative needs an opportunity to try on a situation to see if she can get used to it.

You can point out to her situations where she may want to think things over before she refuses. You might say, "Do you want to call Michelle back tomorrow about the party? That will give you time to think it over."

Eventually, as an adult, she can learn to say things like, "That's an interesting idea. Can I get back to you on that?"

COPING WITH TRANSITIONS

Changing gear from one activity to another is particularly difficult for children who are sensitive to change. And that can make getting through the day hard on everyone. Just getting your child out of bed, dressed, fed, to school, in from play, through the homework hour, and back to bed can feel like running a marathon. Here are some techniques:

• Give your sensitive child advance warning before any change. Instead of making her do something right that minute, give her just a bit of slack:

"In five minutes, it will be time to get out of the pool."

"At the next commercial, please bring down your clothes hamper."

"Three more swings, then jump off and we'll get in the car."

- Set a timer and place it near your child as she is winding down an activity. That way she begins the process of reminding herself of an upcoming change of scene. You could also use a wind-up toy, a music box, or a short piece of taped music.
- For an older child especially, let her pick a stopping point whenever possible. She might want to finish her picture before she has to clean up her paints. Or she may have one page left of a chapter. She'll be more able to make a change when you let her have some say. Once she's picked one, however, do hold her to it.
- Budget more time for transitions and warnings than you would with your other children.
- Use imagination and humor to ease transitions. The horsey ride up the stairs to bed is a time-honored way to make transitions more palatable. So is putting the toy animals to bed before taking a nap, or buckling up into the space ship (car seat) and blasting off on Saturday morning errands. Whenever you keep the fun in daily routines, you ease the intensity of the transition.
- Let your child know ahead of time about any change in plans. Sensitive children sometimes react negatively if the dinner menu changes. If you

told your child you would go to the bank, the shoe store, and the ice-cream store, she may get upset if you change the order. Show your respect for her need to prepare herself.

- Resist the temptation to avoid conflict by avoiding all structure and scheduling. Eric may dislike having to go to a new camp every week, but it's good for him to have to get used to *some* camp. Getting your daughter to bed at a reasonable hour may be a challenge, but she won't benefit from having no scheduled bedtime at all.

THE SENSITIVE CHILD AND DISCIPLINE

There she stands, your littlest angel, the tender-foot you instinctively want to protect. She gazes soulfully up at you, lower lip quivering, uprooted houseplants sprinkled all around. Your sensitive three-year-old has misbehaved, and you really ought to throw the book at her. And yet, look at her there, so fragile, so . . .

Your sensitive child needs limits and discipline like any other child. As we outlined in Chapter Five, one of the most common (and understandable) missteps the parents of sensitive children make is to go too easy on them, be afraid to set limits. The outcome can be a child who is not only sensitive, but manipulative and unruly as well. Hardly what we want for our kids.

Ironically, sensitive children tend to accept limits more readily than most children, and this can make discipline issues deceptively simple. "I just have to look at him funny and he stops misbehaving and starts crying," says Josh's father.

This compliance can be a blessing at times. But it's possible for sensitive children to become over-compliant and unable to state their needs and assert their rights and opinions. It's also possible for them to cultivate and dramatize their sensitivity in such a way that they avert punishment.

One emotionally sensitive eight-year-old is adept at diverting attention from her own misbehavior to her feelings about being reprimanded.

Samantha is deliberately distracting her six-year-old brother during the most challenging level of his Space Invaders video game, causing him to crash in defeat. Her brother screams in protest, and their father intervenes. "Now, why did you do that, Samantha? You ruined Brad's game. That wasn't very nice."

Samantha runs to her mother. "Daddy hurt my *feelings!*" she wails.

Then there's eleven-year-old Roger, who reacts dramatically to any criticism. "I'm hopeless! I'm terrible! You don't love me! I'll run away! I might as well kill myself!"

Those statements are not unusual in all children, but in sensitive children, they can carry considerable weight with parents.

Earlier in this chapter, we discussed the importance of managing behavior, not temperament. That's true in matters of discipline as well. Samantha's mother might say, "You chose to bother Michael during his game. That meant Dad had to break up the fight. I can see that your feelings are hurt, and we can talk about that later when we've all calmed down."

Generally, however, sensitive children accept limits fairly easily. Here's why:

- Sensitive children often have a fondness for predictability, which makes it easier for them than for most children to remember rules.
- Similarly, sensitive children are more likely than other children to look before they leap, to stop and think before they act.
- Sensitive children are more likely to worry about future events, and about their own adequacy.
- Sensitive children often have a powerful desire to please and to avoid disappointing those they love.

FIVE TECHNIQUES FOR SENSITIVE DISCIPLINE

The general suggestions above for coping with sensitivity can be applied to matters of setting limits, as well. Here are some additional pointers:

1. Use assertive, rather than punitive, discipline. That means you convey to your child that you, as the adult, are willing and able to set reasonable limits on your child's behavior. You will explain the rules and the consequences, and enforce them with consistency and kindness.

2. Focus on the behavior, not the sensitivity. Naturally you will take into account your child's sensitivity as you establish expectations and consequences. But when you reprimand or correct your child, you won't say, "I see that you have trouble with transitions." That discussion is better conducted when you're not in enforcement mode.

   Instead, say, "The rule is no television before homework is done. Please turn it off and go back and finish your work."

   If your shy ten-year-old has remained mute when you tried to introduce her to one of your friends, you can say, "You're able to shake hands and greet adults respectfully. Please do it when we see Mr. Arthur next time."

3. Similarly, focus on the behavior, not the motive. When you're setting limits, you need to concentrate on what your child has done, rather than on why she has done it. Suppose your son has rudely rejected the food offered by his hostess. You know that he is a picky eater, bothered by strong flavors. You understand this, but that doesn't give him permission to be rude.

   After you've discussed his rude behavior and its consequences, you can renew your discussions of his sensitivity when the discipline issue is over. You can tell him you understand why he feels like behaving the way he does, but that he has to find acceptable ways to behave.

4. Be specific. If you say, "Be good! Be a good girl!" that's hard enough for any kid to visual-

ize. A sensitive child may anguish over what it means to be good, and all the possible ways that she might not make the grade. Far better to say, "Remember, no talking in the movie" or "This is a 'no touch' store."

5. Keep punishments short and sweet. Chances are that your sensitive child is more responsive to your disapproval and to punishment than another child might be. Especially if your child is emotionally sensitive, you'll find that a little goes a long way.

The most effective punishments are consistent and short. If you issue a time-out when your four-year-old breaks a house rule about snacks in the living room, a few minutes should be as effective as a half hour.

GOOD-BYE, BOSS. HELLO, CONSULTANT

Your sensitive child will always be sensitive, and she will always be your child. But someday, she will be an adult, an independent person who is capable of doing for herself many of the things you do for her now.

When that time comes, she will also handle the management of her own sensitivity by herself. She will

- understand,
- respect,
- comfort,

- inspire,
- encourage, and
- forgive herself.

And just as a small child she learned to stretch herself up to the counter and ask the clerk for a vanilla ice-cream cone, your child will learn, over time, to explain her sensitivity and her needs to others. In college, she may propose a small-group project, rather than a major report to the entire class. Or she will explain to her friends that she finds rock concerts stressful, but she'd be happy to join them at a party the next day.

Whenever you talk to your sensitive child in a way that focuses on the behavior at hand, rather than her inadequacies, you make her more open to ways of solving problems and managing on her own. And that is the key to helping her take over the reins of her own sensitivity.

As your sensitive child grows older, you get a whole series of promotions. If you do your job right, you get promoted from nurse to teacher, from foreman to supervisor, from boss to consultant. You become less of a benign dictator and more of a trusted advisor—and, ultimately, a loving parent and good friend of your adult sensitive child.

◆ 7 ◆

Shy Anxiety:
Helping Your Child Cope With Social Distress

This is a book about many dimensions of sensitivity, and shyness is just one form.

But of all those styles, there's nothing quite like shyness—classical, traditional shyness—to generate parental concern, worry, and outright heartache. The image of the shy child is of a small, lonesome little boy or girl, hovering on the periphery of a group of children. We think of a child who just can't get the words out, who never raises his hand, who never reveals his abilities to others.

In its severest manifestation, it is wide-ranging in its impact on a child's future. The extremely shy child may have limited opportunity for relationships, both intimate and social. He may have trouble academically, even if he's quite intelligent, and difficulty in achieving professional success in spite of his abilities. He may become withdrawn and isolate himself from the pleasures and rewards life has to offer.

And it's because shyness is so worrying that we devote this chapter to shyness—what causes it, what it feels like, and how best to manage and reduce it.

IS HE SHY, OR JUST SOLITARY?

As we discussed in Chapter One, the social category of sensitivity covers more than just shyness. It also includes the introverted, independent child who is inwardly directed and prefers being alone.

Like Brandon, the third grader whose after-school routine we observed in Chapter Four, the solitary child genuinely enjoys being alone, and indeed, needs substantial blocks of time for calm reflection. Often, these children occupy themselves with material objects in their solitary play. Brandon draws and colors; other children build models, play imaginary games with Legos and dolls, or, as they grow older, devote themselves to building sets, model kits, science projects, or collections.

These children are socially sensitive and may need special encouragement to venture into social situations and develop the social skills they'll need in life. But they're not really shy.

It's the classically shy child, who is distressed in social or unfamiliar situations, who needs the most attention.

The shy child, ironically, often longs to have friends and to be accepted by a group. But several factors conspire to erect a barrier between this child and his dreams, and he often finds himself isolated against his wishes.

These barriers may include low self-image, general anxiety (not just in social situations), a highly reactive nervous system, and an unwillingness to take risks.

Certainly, the solitary child can fail to develop the social skills that every child needs, due to lack of interest and practice. If your child fits that description, you'll need to gently encourage opportunities for friendship and social growth, no matter how happy your child may be by himself.

But it's the shy child who suffers the most and is at greatest risk of lingering effects from his sensitive temperament.

Brandon, the third-grade boy who needs solitude to restore his emotional reservoirs, is typical of the socially sensitive children who manage well. But Alexis, the girl who is afraid to speak in class, may experience long-term effects, including poor academic performance.

Or consider five-year-old Ramon. When his father went to pick him up at a new friend's house, the friend's mother informed him that Ramon had wet his pants. "I don't know why he didn't just ask to use the bathroom," she said. To her, it was inconceivable that this pleasant child, who seemed to play happily with her son, was so anxious about making a request of an adult that he would risk the major humiliation of wet pants.

WHAT SHYNESS LOOKS LIKE

"I can tell who the shy kids are going to be on the first day," says a kindergarten teacher. "They come in clinging, with their heads down. They don't make eye contact. I know they're going to need a lot more time to adjust than the other ones."

Even in later grades, the shy child typically stands out in class.

"My daughter, a third grader, is very bright, but she absolutely will not speak in class," says a mother. "She has so much to offer, but she won't let people know about her gifts. Even when she knows the answer, even when the teacher calls on her, she refuses to answer."

As we saw in Chapter Two, shy children have predictable behaviors and physiological traits. These qualities reveal themselves to researchers (not to mention prom dates and audiences) in classical ways, like blushing, perspiring, speechlessness or stammering, the failure to look others in the eye, and a stooped or stiff body stance.

These traits are nearly universal among shy children, and among most people who aren't shy, during occasional moments of self-consciousness. They are difficult to overcome because they are grounded in physiology, associated with the physical responses to fear, anxiety, or threat.

There are internal measures as well, that indicate

the physiological experience of shyness. As we discussed in Chapter Two, they include changes in adrenaline activity, heart rate, and blood pressure.

When inhibited or shy children feel threatened, as they often do in unfamiliar situations, they may demonstrate the same protective reactions that are observed in animals: The baby rabbit "freezes"; the two-year-old stands rooted to the spot. The young monkey stares at the unfamiliar monkey; the shy preschooler stares with round, wary eyes at an unfamiliar child.

WHAT SHYNESS FEELS LIKE

Just as ordinary, rational fears can become phobias, ordinary, rational caution can take on a phobic dimension. Extreme shyness is similar to a social phobia.

Consider Adam, a shy nine-year-old who dreads speaking out in class. During the first week of school, the teacher tried to encourage the kids to get acquainted by having them stand up and tell something about themselves and their interests. When Adam's turn came, he was mortified. He couldn't think of anything to say, and when he tried to speak, his words were inaudible. He wished he were anywhere but standing there in front of that hostile audience.

Now, Adam dreads school because he worries that his teacher will ask him to speak again, and he'll relive the entire experience.

All his symptoms—butterflies in the stomach, blushing, sweaty palms—don't wait for the occasion itself. They kick in as soon as he even *thinks* about it.

Classically shy children may have a strong negative perception of their own worth, and their own skills. They may be quite shrewd in realizing, often from an early age, that they are not able to do or say the things that more socially adept children do and say.

Often shy children feel so focused on the frightening aspect of a social situation that they have little energy left for the activity itself. When that happens, their actual performance is less polished than it might have been, and their prophecies of doom are more likely to be fulfilled.

Interestingly, studies comparing two kinds of socially unpopular children—extremely shy kids and aggressive children—indicate that the shy children have a lower opinion of themselves than do children whose unpopularity is related to aggressive, antisocial behavior.

Clearly, whatever the cause or origin of shyness, an essential approach to easing it is to help the child change that negative perception.

SHYNESS AS EXPERIENCE

Our premise in this book is that sensitivity has a significant biological, and probably genetic, base. But even the most enthusiastic booster of behavioral genetics would not attribute *all* of this behavior to immutable traits present from birth.

That means that to a considerable degree, the child's environment can contribute to shyness and make it more intense, or ease it and generate more positive ways of getting on in life.

Let's consider some of the elements that may contribute to shyness, or exacerbate shyness in a child who already has a temperamental bias toward sensitivity. (Just because you have a shy child, of course, does not mean you match any of these descriptions.)

- Parental style may have an effect on making shyness more or less intense. Generally, a strict and punitive parental style exacerbates shyness, while a loving but firm approach is more positive.
- Some shy children have parents who are themselves either shy or highly anxious.
- Children who grow up in either geographical or social isolation may be shy because they have not had adequate opportunity to become comfortable with other children or to practice social skills.
- Many children who may or may not have a temperamental bias toward shyness experience shyness at certain tension-filled stages in their lives: starting school, starting college, and—probably the most common—early adolescence.
- Some children exhibit shyness only in certain circumstances and situations. For more detail on particular times and places where shyness can be a problem, see Chapter Eight.

- Parents who are highly critical and judgmental can enhance shyness in their child, even if the critical remarks are directed at others. An atmosphere of intolerance has a negative effect on children's confidence.
- Repeated labeling of a shy child seems to increase shy behavior.
- A home environment that criticizes mistakes and demands perfection and success is likely to discourage risk-taking in children. Thus, potentially shy children do not get the chance to practice and improve their risk-taking skills.

SOME IRONIES OF SHYNESS

"My daughter has a terrible time with any spontaneous experience. She's completely paralyzed if she has to be introduced to someone, and she absolutely hates to use the telephone. Yet she can stand up in front of the whole school and give a speech with no trouble at all. That completely mystifies me. Other kids who are really outgoing freeze when they get before a group, but my shy daughter does very well."

The phenomenon of shyness is full of ironies, and shy children are full of surprises. No wonder we parents so often zig when we should zag as we try to help our sensitive children!

Actually, the child described above is quite typical. Although many shy children would collapse under the pressure of a public performance, a surprising number do quite well. The reason appears to be the *predictability* of the setting. A performance, a recital, or a speech generally allows the performer a degree of control. She can practice her music, rehearse her lines, or memorize her remarks.

What usually upsets these children is spontaneous interaction, like introductions to strangers and dating situations.

Another way that shy children may surprise us is in the intensity of their need for the company and approval of others. They often are less independent, more dependent on others, and less likely to be comfortable in solitude, than average children. Unlike solitary children, who tend to be comfortable by themselves, shy children usually want very much to be accepted by a group.

Shy children often have trouble being tolerant of others, just as they may be overcritical of themselves. They may not taunt or openly criticize others, but they can be judgmental. Eventually, when they do interact socially, their intolerant tone may lead to further rejection from others.

HELPING YOUR SHY CHILD

There are ways to help your shy child blossom, as we discussed in the last chapter. Following are techniques that address the specific needs of genuinely shy children.

Whether your child's shyness seems to have a

persistent basis in temperament, or if it just crops up in certain situations, the same general points apply: You'll want to boost your child's sense of worthiness, encourage an attitude of spontaneity, and teach specific social skills and tricks of the trade.

We divide these suggestions into two parts: those that have to do with attitude and self-image, and those that involve nuts-and-bolts skills.

How to help: Attitude

- Remember the importance of labels. Avoid labeling your child as shy and discourage others from doing so as well. If a neighbor or relative says, "Oh, isn't she shy!" you might say (in your child's hearing), "Well, Audrey likes to take her time in new situations. I'm sure she'll be more willing to talk later."
- Try to discourage your child from describing himself as shy, but do it tactfully.

   Preschool age children usually understand what shyness is, and may describe themselves that way—especially if other adults call them shy. With a child that age, you can just say, "I wouldn't call you 'Shy.' I'd call you '*Steven!*' And Steven likes to wait until he knows people before he talks."

   As your child grows older, continue to encourage him to describe himself in ways that focus on his strengths, not his perceived weaknesses. If your son says he had trouble giving his book report because "I'm too shy," you might respond, "Well, I know you didn't feel comfortable giving your report to the class. But you're the kind of kid who likes to be prepared. The more practice you get, the easier it will be for you."

- Similarly, use the same techniques for gently discouraging the kind of self-fulfilling prophecies shy children sometimes use: "I'll never be able to do this," "Nobody will come to my party," "I'll just mess up as usual."

You'll need to discourage the negatives and accentuate the positives in a constructive way, however. Rather than say, "Oh, don't be silly. Of course you can," you might offer to your child positive statements he can use himself: "I'm having trouble because this is really hard! Nobody can do this the first time!"

- Remember that shy children need love, affection, and praise as much as (and maybe more than) other children, even though they may be less likely to ask for it. Find every opportunity to cuddle, hug, adore, and admire your shy child (taking care not to go overboard or put him on the spot).

The trick is to find ways of praising a shy child that do not "spotlight" him. The best way is to focus on the child's accomplishment, rather than on him. You might say, "Greg, that's a neat painting. I like the way you made the houses different colors, like a rainbow. Grandma would really love this one. If you'd like, we can send it to her."

- Since shy children are often overly concerned about "messing up," try to desensitize your child by "practicing" failure.

  Even very young children can share in the silliness of putting the puzzle pieces in upside down. As children get older, you can see who can draw the silliest picture or make the messiest scribble or the lumpiest piece of clay. Anything that steers your child away from perfectionism helps him in this task.

- Model a tolerance for your own imperfections. You can tell a young child about all the things you did wrong as a child, or as an adolescent, and how the world didn't come to an end. You survived.

- Encourage rational risk-taking. Try to create an environment in which failure loses its importance. You started that with "practicing" failure, effectively taking the sting out through play and laughter. Now, you neutralize failure further by encouraging an attitude of "Why not! It's worth a try!"

  Encourage your child to try new tasks, and then reward the attempt, rather than the outcome. If your child tries to climb to the top of the apple tree but only gets halfway up, you can say, "Wow! You climbed higher than ever before!"

- Tell stories in which your child is the hero who solves the mystery, saves the world, rescues the prince or princess, or whatever. Let your child direct the story line. Because it's fantasy, anything is possible.

- Once your child is past the early elementary years and is more capable of thinking analytically about the challenges he faces, you can encourage reasonable risk-taking by helping him examine all the possible outcomes of a daunting situation.

  Suppose, for example, your son is concerned about inviting guests to his party, being in a play, or going to a crowded family picnic. Help him outline all the possible outcomes of his effort, including the ones he hopes for (my friends will all come to my party) and the ones he fears (I'll get sweaty and forget my lines). Even worst-case scenarios hold less power when they're viewed as one of several possible outcomes.

- Some children benefit from relaxation techniques. Before a daunting task, your child might try visualizing a completely restful, safe, and comfortable setting, then visualize himself feeling just as relaxed in the situation he fears.

- Model tolerance. If your child hears nothing but judgmental criticism when you discuss others, thinking the worst of everything people do, he may fear that you are as critical of him. Demonstrate to him that you can give other people the benefit of the doubt.

- Provide opportunities for service and being helpful. Helping others allows the child to redirect the focus off himself, and toward the person being helped. Even such simple things as, "Grandpa left his glasses on the porch. Would you get them for him?" (and a genuine thank you after) convey this message.

- Finally, be realistic about the changes you expect from your child, even as you practice these attitude-improving techniques. Don't expect miracles. Accept that your child may never have quite the spontaneous confidence that less-sensitive children have. Rather, look at the progress that he actually makes and point it out to him. By easing your child into a more tolerant way of viewing himself, and by building his confidence that he can, eventually, achieve his goals, you will have added immeasurably to his capacity to succeed.

How to help: Skills

If your shy child is able to build his self-esteem, his confidence, and his comfort with risk, he'll make great progress. But he'll do much better if he also learns simple ways of easing his social interactions.

- Rehearse. You and your child can role-play and rehearse everything from looking someone in the eye when speaking, to conducting a conversation on the telephone, to preparing for the talent show.
- Teach your child ways to approach another child, or a group of children. Socially effective preschoolers know how to approach a group physically, to wait for a point of entry, and to engage others in conversation. Your child can practice

phrases like, "What are you doing?" and "Can I build over here?" and "I'll be the fireman."

- Older children can rehearse conversation skills. Help your child identify short questions or statements that he might use to get conversations going, such as, "Are you playing soccer this year?" or "That math test was hard."

  Teach phrases that *keep* conversations going. If someone asks, "How are you?" your child might be in the habit of mumbling "Okay," and letting the conversational ball drop. Teach some alternatives: "Fine, thanks. How are you doing?"

- Have your child practice some standard greetings, openers and closers. Shy children often avoid saying "Hello" to people, because they don't know precisely what to say. Practice hearty hellos and good-byes, and include some informal ones, like "See ya later, alligator" or "Ciao!" Don't, of course, urge your child to use phrases that feel unnatural to him.

- Give your shy child time to respond to questions and be able to return the conversational ball. Until he learns to be more at ease, he may need time to answer questions.

- At the same time, help him improve his speed by playing rhyming games or word games that require a quick, unrehearsed response.

- If your child is teased because of a particular behavior, do see if it can be eliminated. Thumb-sucking, for example, can invite teasing. Work as your child's partner on ways to eliminate these behaviors. But make it clear to your child that the teaser, not the shy child, is the one at fault for the teasing situation.

- Do arrange play group opportunities so your child can practice social skills and develop friendships. Keep play groups small and in even numbers, to avoid the risk of one child (usually the shyest) being left out.
- Arrange a playdate with a child who is younger than your shy child. This arrangement gives shy kids a chance to be the more skilled member of a pair, to be admired and to experience social mastery.
- Have your child practice looking people right in the eye, even if he doesn't feel ready to speak to them. When you go out, ask him, "What color eyes did that clerk have?"
- Provide opportunities for your child to be "on stage" in safe settings. With his consent, you might ask him to play the piano for one relative or neighbor. Encourage him, beforehand, by reminding him how much pleasure the performance will give the other person. Afterward, praise and reward him, but don't praise excessively.
- Practice phone calls. For some children, talking to a stranger on the telephone is less stressful than approaching a stranger face-to-face. For some children, calling an office or theater for information is easier than telephoning someone socially.
- Point out progress. Say, "Last year, I don't think you would have felt comfortable making that phone call (or ordering in a restaurant, or what-

ever). You've been practicing, and I can see that it's getting easier for you."

Your efforts may not cure your child of all shyness, but they can help him immeasurably. Certainly, shyness carries with it some risks for future unhappiness: social withdrawal and isolation, difficulties in school, the workplace, romance.

But those risks can be reduced if you help your shy child increase his comfort zone, accept himself, feel both confident and forgiving, and develop the basic social tools he'll need to approach and relate to others.

He may still be shy, but he'll be a shy person who is able to succeed, to take sensible risks, to be a member in good standing of the human family, and to experience his full measure of joy and success.

Many adults who were shy as children, and indeed, who still think of themselves as privately or secretly shy, are happy, successful adults.

"I'm naturally shy and cautious in new situations," says one man. "I really like being around people, and once I get comfortable, I love social activity. But I've always had trouble approaching people and feeling 'safe' enough to talk to them.

"As an adult, I still feel that way inside, but I've taught myself to act braver than I am. I've accepted that it's something I have to do if I'm going to have the life I want. I've learned how to conduct an inner dialog—I tell myself, 'You're nervous now, but after you say hello to this person, it will get easier.'

"And it does!"

Trouble Spots:
Helping Your Sensitive Child Cope With Difficult Moments

In her own home, Andrea is a happy, talkative, involved child. But in her classroom, at church, or at a party, Andrea is a changed child. She is silent and watchful. Her voice, if she uses it at all, becomes quiet and tentative. Like other socially sensitive children, her degree of sensitivity depends on her setting, on the situation she finds herself in.

All children, sensitive or not, behave differently in different settings. Many is the child who is able to sit like a statue in a formal situation, only to morph into a wild child when released into the company of children in the backyard.

But sensitive children are particularly likely to behave differently depending on their circumstances, perhaps because they *are* so susceptible to subtle cues of setting and mood. Exactly what setting gives your child trouble is an individual matter. But there are some common trouble spots that create difficulties for many sensitive children. This chapter is about identifying and coping with those situations.

If temperament is about comfort, then comfort levels vary depending on your child's situation. The cause of discomfort may be an activity, like shopping for clothes, greeting people, or saying good-bye. It may be a physical location, such as the schoolroom, the community swimming pool, an airplane, or the strange bed in a motel room.

Setting, also, is a state of mind. For example, whether a situation is spontaneous or rehearsed makes a difference in how comfortable it feels. Whether it's serious, like a religious ceremony, or all in fun, like an afternoon with a friend. Whether it's work or social.

This is true for adults, as well. As one successful entrepreneur puts it, "I can pick up the phone and call halfway around the world and talk to strangers without any trouble. If it's a business situation, I'm fine. But socially? Forget it. I always have a feeling that I'm imposing when I call people at home. I worry if what I have to ask or say justifies, so I'm more hesitant."

MANAGING SETTING: THE BIG PICTURE

You and your child will be better able to cope with sensitivity if you can recognize trouble spots, plan for them, work around them, and buffer your child when you're in the midst of them.

First, we'll look at two general points, then move

on to specific situations that are particularly difficult for sensitive children to manage.

Buffer the Transitions

Although sensitive-to-change kids have the most trouble with transitions, most sensitive children become upset when settings change too fast or too frequently. Being whisked from day care to Mom's office where she has to finish up some paperwork to the supermarket to home can be too much for any sensitive child. You can't eliminate all transitions, and all changes of setting from your child's life. But it's helpful to schedule her day so that you spare her too many changes of scene.

It's All in the Timing

Sensitive children handle stressful situations better when they are feeling rested, strong, and capable. Your socially sensitive child may be better able to handle a group lesson in the morning, rather than the evening, depending on when she feels more energetic and thus capable. Your sensitive-to-change toddler may better handle a series of Saturday errands in the afternoon, after her nap. When possible, match activities to your child's rhythms of energy and fatigue.

The time element is important, also, in how long a sensitive child can handle a difficult setting.

There's not too much you can do about the length of the school day, but you can keep other activities short. Trips to the museum and visits to friends' homes are open-ended and can be trimmed so your sensitive child will be able to leave before she is worn-out.

"My daughter was finally ready to go to a birthday party. It was given by one of her newest friends, and she really wanted to give it a try. The girl's mother had rented a musician to come and do children's songs, and she wanted to get her money's worth, so the party lasted four hours. Four hours! My daughter would have had a great time if the party was half that length."

Those situations that are harder to cut short—religious services, movies, or air travel—need to be kept to a minimum and planned with care.

EVERYDAY TROUBLE SPOTS

For most sensitive children, home is the most comfortable setting of all. Yet it's in the daily routines that many sensitive children show their challenging colors.

Clothing and Dressing

SITUATION: You're getting your family ready for a trip to your in-laws' home for Thanksgiving. This is the one time that the whole family gets together, and all the children will be there—dressed in their most adorable outfits. Your seven-year-old daughter says she won't go if she has to wear "anything scratchy." She wants to wear her well-worn fleece jogging outfit and sneakers.

WHAT TO DO: You *could* let your daughter wear what she likes. But you feel it's important that she learn to adapt to social conventions, at least on important occasions that mean a lot to others. So you cut a deal.

You say, "Honey, I know you don't like to dress up, but this is a special occasion and all the kids will be wearing dresses and jackets. I think you should wear a dress, too, but I don't see any reason why you should have to wear it after dinner is over. Why don't we bring along your comfy clothes, and you can change into them later, if you feel like it."

Of course, you've already selected (or helped your daughter select) dress clothing that is as comfortable as it can be. Scratchy taffeta may not be a good choice, but a soft jersey dress in a pretty print might be both appropriate and comfortable.

Other suggestions:

- Your child with low sensory threshold really can feel things pinch, gather, bind, scratch, or tug. Most of the time, it makes sense to go along with her preferences.
- When you shop for a low threshold child, pay as much attention to the insides of the clothes for comfort as to the outside appearance. Check for

smooth seams and linings, and watch out for appliques that have rough stitching on the inside of the garment.

- While your child is young and you do the shopping, choose easy to wear, coordinated, comfortable, simple garments. Stay away from anything fancy, lacy, tight, or binding (except for getting christened, confirmed, bar mitzvahed, or photographed).

- With older children, clothes often become a central issue of conflict in the family. Within reason, allow for your sensitive child's unconventional tastes. Battles arise between parent and child about what to buy, and what outfits are acceptable for particular outings. Children with low sensory threshold may refuse to wear coats on cold days; emotionally sensitive children may dread standing out in a crowd because their clothes are different from the norm.

- For small children, getting dressed brings with it a dozen opportunities to be frustrated. Sleeves get stuck inside out. Shoes seem to go on the wrong feet. Buttons plot to go in the wrong holes, if they go in at all. Allow a sensitive child extra time for dressing so she isn't rushed.

Mealtime

SITUATION: You're trying to get the family to sit down for dinner, but your sensitive child is resisting. He wants to finish his television program before he joins the family. When he drags himself into the kitchen, he complains that his brother has switched chairs and is using "his" chair. He doesn't like what's being served. You're beginning to lose your patience.

WHAT TO DO: This particular meal may be a lost cause, but try a different approach the next day. You say, "Matthew, last night there were lots of things about dinner that you didn't like. Tonight, we're going to try something different. You're going to help pick out what we have, and then you can help me get things ready." Matthew, who is sensitive to change and to anything unexpected, can benefit from knowing exactly what's on the menu. He'll be in control of the seating arrangements and the table settings. And because he'll be involved in preparing the meal, he'll have less trouble making the transition from playtime to mealtime.

Of course, Matthew won't always select what the family has for dinner. But if he's involved in preparations, he'll bring a more positive attitude to the table.

Mealtime can cause stress with any child, sensitive or not. But if your child has low sensory threshold, or is sensitive to change, like Matthew, the prospect of getting through *one* meal, much less three, can be daunting.

• Try to avoid rushing meals. Children who savor every flavor, or who have trouble with the texture of certain foods, will dawdle. Sensitive-to-change children will balk at every new food. Both kinds of sensitivity can yield pokey eaters.

- When your child is very young, be sensitive to texture and flavor and let her make choices and express preferences.

- Teach older sensitive children ways to reject food politely. You arm your sensitive child for getting on in the world by teaching her to say "No, thank you," rather than "EEEEeeewww!" when she is offered a food she dislikes.

- Children who respond negatively to unfamiliar experiences will need more time to get used to a new food. Don't assume that the first rejection means the food shouldn't be offered again another time.

Bedtime

This is a particularly difficult time of day for children who have low sensory threshold and those who are sensitive to change. Going from wakefulness to sleep is a major transition. For some children, waking up is difficult as well. That's especially true for children who wake up from a nap crabby and out of sorts. As with most aspects of sensitivity, you'll want to do what you can to increase your child's comfort level at bedtime.

- Don't make an issue of pajamas. If your child refuses to wear binding pajamas and complains that the seams bother her, or that he's too hot or too cold, listen to her sensory cues. No one gives out fashion awards for what your child wears to bed.

Older children can determine for themselves what's comfortable—sweatpants, extra long T-shirts, whatever's comfortable. For babies and toddlers, however, there is the issue of fire safety; you'll want to make sure the garment is officially labeled fire retardant so it's safe to wear while sleeping. If your child resists nightgowns, footed sleepers, or pajama sets with snaps, try oversized plain pajama tops.

- A quiet setting is essential for low threshold children. They really do have trouble getting to sleep and staying asleep when there is noise. Similarly, such children are more likely to be awakened by light. Consider getting room-darkening shades for your child's bedroom.

- Allow enough time for a bedtime routine. For very young children, that routine may involve soothing baths, several bedtime stories, lullabies, and hugs. For older children, it may involve a television program, or a play session with quiet toys.

- Do give your child advance warning as bedtime approaches.

FRIENDSHIP AND SOCIAL LIFE

Children who are socially and emotionally sensitive frequently have difficulty forging friendships and feeling comfortable in group settings. They have to learn and practice the social tools and techniques that come easily to more confident children.

SITUATION: You are sitting in the park watching your five-year-old daughter play with two other little girls. As they play in the sandbox and compete for turns on the swings, it becomes clear that the other two are more aggressive than your child, refusing to share space in the sandbox and turns on the swings. Your daughter is growing upset but clearly doesn't know how to handle the situation.

WHAT TO DO: Take your daughter aside for a quiet chat. Begin with your assessment of her feelings. You can say, "I noticed you're not getting much time on the swings. Do you want to swing more?" If she agrees, you can say, "Let's think of some ways to ask for a turn." She can learn to say, "It's my turn to swing now," in a strong, confident voice, rather than stand wistfully by.

Have her watch other children playing and point out what they're doing. "The sandbox is a store, and that girl is selling acorns. Maybe you can go to the store and ask to buy some."

Additionally, she might watch for a toy that nobody is using at the moment and start with that. She might approach another child directly and ask permission to join a game, or she might watch for a "point of entry" into an ongoing game (like riding up on a pretend horse and delivering pretend newspapers to the group).

You may not "solve" this situation on the spot,

since it takes time to build social skills. But every small success builds confidence and paves the way for further successes.

Parties

Sensitive children often have mixed feelings about parties. They may look forward to the fun, but worry about being in a strange home, fret about being embarrassed, or become exhausted by all the activity.

- If your sensitive child really doesn't want to attend a party, it's okay to decline politely.
- If your child would like to attend but is anxious, prepare her for what it will be like.

Sometimes the less obvious solution is best. "I tried helping Marissa handle her shyness by shortening the time she would have to spend at a birthday party," recalls one mother. "I talked to the hostess and explained that Marissa was a bit shy and would it be all right if I brought her late and picked her up early. It seemed like a great idea to me, but it actually backfired. When we dropped her off, the house was in such chaos that Marissa was very clingy and retreated into a shell. She didn't even have a chance to talk to her friend. And when we returned to pick her up, things were still crazy.

"What I'll do next time is ask her friend's parents if Marissa can come *early*, rather than late. That way, she and the birthday girl could help set up. They'd have some one-on-one time before the stressful part of the party begins."

When your sensitive child is the birthday girl, she may have trouble with the present-opening phase of the party. Children who have trouble with transitions, in particular, get stuck. They open one present and want to stop and play with it, ignoring the remaining gifts and the circle of watchful party guests. Many children have difficulty feeling positive about anything they haven't gotten used to. They tend not to show pleasure over their presents, and that can make them seem ungrateful.

If present-opening is a problem, you have several options:

- Keep the party very small so the number of gifts is small.
- Save the gifts to open after the party, then send thank you notes to the guests.
- Teach your child to smile and say "thank you," even if she's not sure she likes something. Practice with her before the party.

AWAY FROM THE NEST

Away from home, you'll need to learn to explain sensitivity to others outside your family. Whether it's your child's teacher or coach, or relatives, you'll need to draw on your positive vocabulary to discuss your child's sensitivity with others. You'll serve as her lawyer and his public relations firm.

Day Care and Nursery School

- Discuss your child's temperament with her new teacher, using positive language that focuses on your child's needs. You might say, "Nicole is quiet and probably won't join in very much at first. If she gets plenty of time to watch what's going on, she'll take part when she's ready."
- If your sensitive child is separating from you for the first time, she'll need more reassurance on the first day than an older or more experienced child might. You'll need to prepare her for the big day, discuss it in a positive way, and reassure her that you will indeed return.
- Some sensitive preschoolers require a gradual approach to separation, in which the parent stays with the child for the first session, then gradually withdraws until the child feels confident on her own. Once that adjustment phase is over, however, departures should be firm, cheerful, and short.

  As one kindergarten teacher says, "Too many parents make their departure too long. They hesitate, come back for one more kiss. The child says, 'Gee, even Mom doesn't want to leave me here.' The parents need to exude confidence that says, 'I'm leaving you in a good place.'"
- For children who are sensitive to change, even

pleasant changes can be a difficult transition. That means that going home from day care or nursery school can be tough. Try to involve the teacher in helping your child prepare for departure. She might remind your child ten minutes ahead of time that you'll be arriving soon. She could set a timer, and she can watch as your arrival grows closer. She can help her finish up whatever she's working on so that she doesn't have to abandon a favorite project when you arrive. She might put out her coat and backpack ahead of time to make the end-of-day transition smoother.

School

School can be a challenging setting for sensitive children for many reasons. There's the constant change, from leaving home, to arriving at school, to changing classrooms, recess, back on the bus, and so on.

There's the social pressure of crowded classrooms, new faces, teasing, the possibility of embarrassment or loneliness.

And there's the anxiety of worrying about performing well, of making mistakes, of forgetting something.

Teachers must, of necessity, cater to a large group of children who have individual temperaments and personalities. There's no way that one teacher can tailor the entire curriculum and schedule to the specific needs of each child. You and your child will have to do some compromising and some coping.

SITUATION: You get a telephone call from your fifth grader's teacher. She says, "Alicia is so shy! I can't get her to participate in class. She does quite well on tests, but her grade won't reflect that unless she begins to contribute."

WHAT TO DO: You thank the teacher for her interest and agree that Alicia's temperament makes it difficult for her to hold her own in class.

You can share with the teacher what you have found helpful at home. "We've found that Alicia will loosen up more when she's comfortable and when she doesn't feel that she's on the spot. She has the hardest time in the fall, when the class and the kids seem so unfamiliar. You'll probably find that she does better in the spring.

"Would it be possible for Alicia to contribute in another way, especially early in the school year when she's most self-conscious? Alicia is friends with Courtney; could they be assigned to give a joint presentation? Or maybe Alicia could contribute by drawing a map on the board, instead of speaking."

Then you talk to Alicia and say: "Mrs. Durand would like to see you participate more in class. I know that's not the easiest thing for you to do, but she's willing to help you any way she can. Here are some ideas we discussed. What do you think?"

Other suggestions for the school setting:

- If your school allows tours or visits in the summer before the school year begins, by all means take your child to see the building, the room (if you know which one it will be), and where the bathrooms and drinking fountains are. Emotionally sensitive children, in particular, benefit from advance visits because they can worry intensely about not being able to find things or getting lost.

- If you know the school and the teachers, pay attention to the fit between teacher and child. Most teachers are adept at dealing with different temperaments among their children, but some are more successful than others. Socially or emotionally sensitive children can find some teachers frightening. Often the teachers are wonderful, energetic, exciting people who are marvelous for most children, but overwhelming to some sensitive children. Other teachers, even with the best of intentions, tend to discipline in loud voices that terrify sensitive kids.

- If you think a particular teacher would be best for your child or would not be a good choice, do let the school principal know—but do so diplomatically. Many school districts either forbid, or strongly discourage, parental requests for a certain popular teacher.

However, most principals and headmasters really do want to find the best setting for each child. You might write the principal a letter in which you explain what your child needs, without making unreasonable demands. It could say, "My son is generally well-behaved and responds well to gentle reminders. He becomes deeply up-set when he is reprimanded sharply. I'd like to ask you to take that into consideration when you make class assignments for next year."

- If your socially sensitive child gets along well with one other child, consider asking if the two children can be assigned to the same class.
- If your child has a low sensory threshold, let your teacher know what your child is particularly sensitive to. You may not want to share the fact that your child refuses to eat waffles if any of the little squares are incomplete, because the syrup leaks. But you would let the teacher know that she has difficulty sorting out important sounds from unimportant ones, and that's why she may seem easily distracted by other children talking, or by sounds from outside the classroom.
- Be aware that for many sensitive children, the most stressful school-related setting is the bus. It's a small, confined space, with several dozen children of varying ages, with minimal supervision as the driver concentrates on the road. Any sensitive child may have great difficulty coping with riding the bus.

"When I realized that the bus was the reason Mark had stomach aches every school morning, I decided to give him a break and drive him for a week," said one mother of a first grader. "It was inconvenient, but it pinpointed the setting that was giving him trouble. Once he didn't have to worry about the noise and teasing on the bus, he started looking forward to school."

- Beware of the transition to junior high or middle school. When children switch from a single classroom and teacher to the secondary pattern of changing rooms and teachers each period, they often feel overwhelmed. Your sensitive child may not be able to avoid seventh grade, but she can enter middle school or junior high with as much preparation and support as you can provide.
- Extracurricular activities, team sports and group lessons share many of the stresses of the school setting. Certainly, sensitive children benefit from these activities, and like all children, they profit from the chance to learn new skills, make new friends, and have a good time.

But do pay close attention to the personality and style of the adult leaders. If the "fit" is poor—if the baseball coach yells too much and scares your son, or if the dance instructor puts too much pressure on your daughter, don't hesitate to take an unhappy child out of a group. If you can't change leaders or coaches, try to find an alternate activity that will provide the benefits and experiences she needs.

Eating Out

Fussy eaters, shrinking violets, and balky complainers don't generally make good dining companions, so restaurant meals can be difficult settings for sensitive children and their families.

- If your child takes time making decisions, find out what's on the menu before a major restaurant outing. Get a copy, or at least be able to mention a few choices so your child can make selections in advance. Remind your child that there may be "specials," so she won't be upset when things aren't exactly as described.

  Even nonsensitive adults can get flustered when the entire group has ordered and they're still trying to digest the menu and make up their minds. It's tougher for a sensitive child who worries about not liking the food, and then has to look up at the waitress and actually open her mouth and speak!

- If the waiting area in your restaurant has video games or amusements, your child may have difficulty leaving the video game to head for the table. Prepare your child in advance about what's going to happen and when.

- Prepare a survival kit for your sensitive child while you wait for the meal to be served. Sensitive children are often receptive to books, crayons and paper, and small quiet toys.

- Limit your restaurant outings to old favorites most of the time if your child is particularly uncomfortable to novelty. However, don't *always* go to familiar places. You can compromise with your child and prepare her to try a new place once in a while.

Shopping and Errands

Errands, especially on weekends, seem to be the foundations of our lives. We have to run out to the store for milk, to drop one of our children at soccer practice, to buy a gift for a friend, to go to the dentist. And often there's no choice but to take a sensitive child along.

- Try to minimize the number of errands and the amount of time you spend on them. An entire Saturday spent racing around town jumping in and out of the car can exhaust anyone, but especially a child who is sensitive to change.
- Establish a car routine. Make sure everyone obeys the rules about seat belts.
- If the question of who gets to sit in the front seat is a contentious issue in your family, establish a schedule. You might rotate turns, make a chart, or—if you have just two children—alternate odd and even days.
- Stores are a prime setting for running into friends and acquaintances who greet your shy child and expect him to speak. These situations aren't avoidable, so do teach your child to practice his greetings. A "hello" and a smile will usually be adequate for young children.
- Run interference for your socially sensitive child if an acquaintance puts her on the spot with lots

of questions. Tactfully intervene and change the subject if your child is distressed.

- Discuss the sequence of the stops you'll make on errand day. "First we'll drop these letters off at the post office. Then we'll go get you some new sneakers. On the way home, we'll stop at the produce stand to buy corn and peaches. Then we'll be home in time for lunch."

Vacations and Trips

Vacations are exciting because they offer the change of scene that so many of us find refreshing and exciting. Yet for children who are sensitive to change, change of scene is work, not play.

They're even harder because they are *supposed* to be fun. Everyone has high expectations for a good time.

- If your child has difficulty falling asleep in an unfamiliar setting, try to pack some familiar nighttime items: her "blankie," a familiar pillow or pillowcase, favorite bedtime books. Don't forget a night-light; fearful children can be panicky when they awaken in the dark in a strange place.
- Remember that you don't have to do it all. Dragging a sensitive-to-change child through the Smithsonian, the Lincoln Memorial, the Capitol, and the National Gallery in one day is a recipe for misery, not happy memories.

- Vacations and family visits are sure to involve crowds, a particularly difficult setting for sensitive children. Schedule some noncrowd days in your vacation. Leave the rest of the family to go shopping one-on-one with your child. If you're touring a bustling metropolis, schedule a day in the countryside for balance.
- Plan ahead for car and airplane trips, especially if your child is anxious about travel or has trouble with change. Explain the itinerary, read books about airplanes, bring survival kits with books, toys, and familiar items from home.
- Greeting people is a particularly difficult moment for sensitive children. When relatives see your child, they may want to pounce and grab, prompting your child to withdraw and getting the whole visit off on the wrong foot.
- When visiting relatives, try for open communication about your child's sensitivity. You can say, "I'm not sure if Michael will be able to handle sightseeing for too long. Maybe we can take him to the Liberty Bell but let him stay at home with me while the rest of you go to the museum."
- Try to schedule "naps" for your child who becomes upset when events move too fast or too many people crowd into her world. Your child doesn't necessarily have to sleep but could be put in a quiet room with a book for an hour.

SPECIAL SITUATIONS

Sensitive children find it particularly difficult to adjust to any change in routine or in the makeup of the household. If the family moves to a new house or Mom gets a new job with different hours, the sensitive child will require plenty of preparation and understanding.

When Grandpa moves in, or houseguests come for a week, or step-siblings come for the summer, it's particularly difficult for sensitive children to keep their cool.

Your sensitive child—like all children—will require extra attention when a new baby enters the family. Children who are sensitive to emotion or sensitive to change will, understandably, have a difficult time adjusting.

When parents divorce, children often find themselves spending part of their time with a noncustodial parent, or sharing their own home with half-siblings who visit. The change and readjustment involved can be difficult whether it's a weekend visit or an entire summer. Children who are socially sensitive find their privacy invaded; emotionally sensitive children pick up on tensions between parents and between a parent and a stepchild. And children who are sensitive to change, naturally, find the change of scenery and characters daunting.

Tasha, a socially sensitive ten-year-old, is devastated every time her twelve-year-old half sister comes on visitation. They have to share a room, and the presence of another person twenty-four hours a day is terribly distressing to Tasha, even though she genuinely likes her sister.

In these situations, parents of sensitive children need—once again—to strike a balance between buffering the child from distress, and encouraging her to master his difficulties. Some suggestions:

- Prepare your child ahead of time for the arrival of visitors, or for visits she will make.
- Discuss house rules and expectations openly, and allow your sensitive child to have an input in this discussion.
- If either the host child or the visiting child is socially sensitive and needs privacy, find a way to provide that. If the children have to share a room, designate another quiet space for the child to retreat on occasion. Or, schedule some activities apart, so the child has some time alone to recharge.

◆ 9 ◆

Looking Ahead:
What the Future Holds for Your Sensitive
Child

"My daughter is very quiet. She keeps her thoughts to herself. I keep trying to get her to open up, to share her concerns with me, but she doesn't. I've accepted this and try not to press her. But my main concern is, will she be able to talk to us if something is really wrong?"

"He falls apart at the tiniest little thing. How will he ever handle the real world?"

"I'm sure she'll be a good citizen, but will she be happy?"

"My son only eats apple slices and my chicken soup. How can he possibly cope when he grows up and moves out on his own?"

"Yesterday at the swimming pool, my four-year-old had just gotten into the water and he said,

'Wait, my leg itches.' He climbed all the way out of the pool to scratch his leg, then he got back in. Meanwhile, his brother and his friends were already splashing around, having a great time. My son is like this all the time. I just can't picture him ever having a good time."

WHAT PARENTS WORRY ABOUT

All parents wonder about what the future holds for their children, whether those children are sensitive or not. Will they manage to get through college—or get *into* college? Can they be trusted to drive a car safely? Will they have friends, fall in love, earn a living, succeed, be happy?

But the parents of sensitive children have more specific worries. Their kids are not the tough, swaggering, street-smart survivors, and they tend not to be among the most socially adept. Parents of sensitive children worry most about their children's relationships, and their fundamental happiness.

- Will my son always be a follower?
- Will my daughter become more assertive?
- How will my child cope with the stresses of adolescence?
- I can't imagine my child surviving a broken love affair.
- How will he ever survive a job interview?
- Will my child's feelings always be hurt so easily?
- Will my son learn to stand up for himself?

Sometimes, parent anxiety is greater when the parent and child share the same kind of sensitivity, and the parent recalls suffering because of it. "He's so much like me. I don't want him going through the same garbage," said a mother whose son, like her, is emotionally sensitive.

As we discussed in Chapter Three, parents worry that their child will suffer the same loneliness they did, or miss out on pleasurable experiences because of shyness or fear.

Parents also worry when they are strikingly different from their sensitive children. "I've always been outgoing, and that served me well in adolescence," says a father. "But my son is so easily discouraged. How will he ever ask a girl out on a date?"

Parents who are consumed with anxiety about their children's future probably have a harder time concentrating on the steps they can take in the present to help their children. In addition, too much parental fretting can convey additional anxiety to their children.

The parents who worry least, and are thus in the best position to parent positively, are those who are either similar in temperament to their children and comfortable with that temperament, or who have come to understand, work with, and even celebrate their sensitive child's individuality, even when child and parent are quite different.

*　　*　　*

"Amanda is shy, but she really does enjoy herself once she feels safe," said one mother who describes her five-year-old daughter as "exactly like me. I'm not at all anxious about her future. She'll be just fine."

"I'm completely unaware of the things my son notices," said a mother of a perceptive son who has low sensory threshold. "When he shares his observations, it's a real treat. Yesterday, he showed me the shimmering rainbow effect on the surface of a puddle in the street. Then he said it reminds him of the wing on the butterfly he caught last weekend."

Daniel, an emotionally sensitive child who has learned to discuss sensitivity comfortably, was preparing to go for a bicycle ride with his less-sensitive mother. As she grumbled about how difficult it was to inflate her bike tires, nine-year-old Daniel waited, then said—calmly and pleasantly—"Mom, you're stressed. I've looked forward to this trip and I'd like you to try to cheer up."

Daniel's mother was surprised and pleased at her son's ability to recognize her emotional state and articulate its effect on him.

"I realized after that that he's going to draw strength from his sensitivity," she says. "He picks up on things that other people don't, but he can speak up about what's going on."

Sometimes, the worries we have about our sensitive children can be eased as they demonstrate their strengths. As they grow, they grow stronger—not always in ways that we are familiar with, but in their own unique way. Consider David's mother's story:

"My son is sensitive to change. He has trouble with transitions, especially—of course—if they require him to change from something he enjoys to something he isn't very interested in doing. Things like homework and chores are a constant battle for us.

"One night I got terribly upset because David had a fifth grade science project due the next day. He was supposed to design and build a machine that would actually run, but without any power source. And he hadn't even *begun!*

"I knew that David is persistent, but he has trouble getting started. I was convinced he'd never get this project done. I have to work on a project in manageable doses. I start and stop and do a lot of pacing. I was projecting my style on him.

"He finally got going around seven o'clock. He kept plugging away, sawing wood and gluing pieces together. I was jumping around, worrying, and he kept going and going and going. He finished at eleven that night. Then he gave me an 'I told you!' smile and collapsed in bed. His project got Best of Category."

David's study habits may leave something to be desired, but they do demonstrate that sometimes our children's differences from us can be as wondrous and rewarding as their similarities to us. Your sensitive child may develop in ways that mystify you, or that worry you. But sensitive children who have confidence in their strengths can often surprise us in their ability to find a style that serves them well.

ASPECTS OF SENSITIVITY THAT ARE LIKELY TO PERSIST

As we've said throughout this book, temperament and sensitivity are such fundamental components of personality that they are likely to persist throughout life, although they can be significantly moderated. The kinds of experiences that feel comfortable, and the tendencies to respond in certain ways to experience, are probably basic building blocks of who we are.

- Sensory threshold is likely to endure. Heightened sensitivity to color, texture, flavor, and sound are, most likely, related to basic brain functions and not subject to major change.
- Social sensitivity will persist to a lesser degree. Although the shyest children often remain shy as they grow older, shyness can be eased significantly.

Jerome Kagan, an authority on temperament, conducted extensive studies of temperament and its persistence in children. He and his colleagues report that among extremely shy eighteen-month-olds, about half are still extremely shy at age eight, and the rest fall into the average range.

That would suggest that the behavior of these highly inhibited children can be modified by experience.

That contrasts with a group of uninhibited and outgoing toddlers. Of that group, 75 percent exhibit the same traits at age eight. A bold, extroverted temperament is more likely to persist than an inhibited, fearful temperament—further evidence that sensitivity can be modified by experience.

Another study examined the behavior of shy children at the age of thirty three months, and again at six years. The early shyness was more likely to persist in boys than it was in girls.

The conclusion might be that if you are the parent of a shy, timid two-year-old, it's anybody's guess whether he'll be shy and timid by the time he's in elementary school. He may be average, he may remain shy, or he may be anywhere in between, depending on how his sensitivity has been handled.

- Emotional sensitivity may persist, but it does not necessarily translate into fear and anxiety. In adulthood, this style of sensitivity may show itself more as intuition and empathy.

  However, extreme fearfulness early in life can suggest a greater susceptibility to phobias and anxiety disorders later in life.

- Resistance to change and novelty may persist throughout life as a tendency to be careful and cautious in new situations.

ASPECTS OF SENSITIVITY THAT OFTEN MODIFY WITH TIME

Although temperament persists throughout life, its influence recedes somewhat in adulthood because it must compete with environment and experiences. The newborn baby is largely a biological creature. But a twenty-five-year-old man is, whatever his innate temperament, to a great degree a product of his history.

By adulthood, we have either learned techniques for managing our temperament biases, or we have not. But ideally, we accommodate ourselves to our temperament just as water accommodates itself to the vessel in which it is held.

If you work with your child's temperament to celebrate his sensitivity at the same time you encourage him to enlarge his skills, you may find that some of these qualities can be modified over time.

- Social sensitivity can be modified with practice and encouragement. Many sensitive adults continue to experience underlying discomfort in social situations but can cope well enough that the sensitivity does not limit them.
- The uncomfortable aspects of emotional sensitivity, as we discussed above, can be eased somewhat. Anxieties and fears can be managed, leaving the more positive dimensions of empathy and caring.
- Some aspects of sensitivity to change can be man-

aged. Most children who have difficulty with adaptability are capable of learning to manage this trait. They may always feel cautious in new situations. But they can learn the skills that help them manage transitions, and they can learn ways of trying new things on their own terms.

If you have a sensitive child now, you will in all likelihood have a sensitive adult offspring in years to come. Temperament does endure. But how it persists, and in what form, is what you can influence. That's what this book has been all about.

THE SENSITIVE ADOLESCENT

Adolescence is a challenging stage of life for any child and that child's parents. But the parents of sensitive children worry more than most. How, they wonder, will my child deal with the pressures, stresses, worries, and heartaches of being a teenager?

- How will my emotionally sensitive teenager handle the disappointments of love and dating?
- How will my child adjust to college and to being away from the routine of home?
- How will my child have the fortitude to apply for a job and enter the workforce? How will she respond when the boss criticizes his work?
- How will my child stand up to peers who try to influence him in harmful ways?

Sensitive teenagers do tend to worry more than most, to become anxious, to play out minor bad experiences into major anguish. Yet others blossom in their high school years and seem less anxious as they see their own skills and capabilities growing. It's helpful to separate the ways that sensitivity makes adolescence more challenging, and then take a look at the way it can enrich that stage of life.

- A sensitive adolescent may find it difficult to take reasonable risks and sample positive experiences: joining an organization, taking up a hobby, studying a foreign language, trying out for a team.
- An emotionally sensitive high school student is more likely than another teen to worry about his friends and take their troubles to heart.
- A socially sensitive teen may avoid many of the group activities which, to the rest of the world, define adolescent pleasure.
- A sensitive-to-change adolescent may remain in an unsatisfactory relationship for reasons of comfort and familiarity, rather than true love.

But sensitivity confers advantages during adolescence as well:

- Shy teenagers may delay dating and romantic relationships, but they do eventually manage them. They may take more time to be sure of their feelings before making commitments, a trait that is hardly negative.

- An adolescent teenager who thinks before he acts, who reflects on the likely outcome of an action before he takes the plunge, avoids many dangers that threaten children and terrify their parents.
- A sensitive adolescent may be a good listener whose ability to tune in to the emotions of others attracts friends and earns respect.
- Sensitive adolescents often find that the perceptiveness and awareness they've had all along blossoms into specific strengths and talents during these years. They may be particularly creative, independent, artistically talented, socially conscious, kindhearted, and empathic.

As we discussed earlier, your child will gradually assume more of the tasks of managing his own sensitivity as he matures. In adolescence, your role changes, too: When he needs advice and support, he will turn as much to his peers as he does to you.

While your child is young, you can work on helping him establish a support system, a network of acquaintances and friends. This system does not need to be extensive (for many children, one or two close friends are adequate).

When he's older, he may blossom socially or he may not. It's not necessary for a child to be "popular," in the usual teenage sense. He doesn't need to have lots of friends in school, be elected to anything, be a member of an athletic team or school club. His support system might be members of a church group, or a few teenagers who enjoy working with computers. He may join the track team, where he experiences affiliation, while still working as an individual. In one community, sensitive, creative teenagers hang out at poetry readings instead of at the mall.

WHEN TO WORRY ABOUT YOUR SENSITIVE CHILD

There is research that suggests that unusually fearful, anxious toddlers are more likely to become adults with anxiety disorders in later life. These disorders include general anxiety, phobias, and panic attacks. Naturally, these are conditions that we hope our children can avoid, since they not only are unpleasant but severely limit people's lives. There are therapists who specialize in treating phobias and anxiety disorders, and that treatment is often quite successful.

Excessive Fears

Your child may be more fearful than other children, as part of his temperament birthright. But fears can become so disabling that they are no longer normal. You'll want to seek help if:

- Your child's fears are so pervasive that he seems never to be free of them.
- Fear seems to prevent your child from functioning in everyday life, enjoying ordinary pleasures,

and seeking ordinary experiences. A child who is afraid to attend school, who refuses to seek out any friendship, who dreads outings and vacations, who refuses to take any risks whatever may need help.

- Your child is suffering from true phobias, rather than ordinary childhood fears. Normal fears are generally manageable and deal with rational concerns. If your child is frightened of clowns at age three, or is afraid of getting shot at age six, or of giving a school presentation at age nine, these are typical childhood fears. If, however, your child's fears take over his life—if he's so worried about war, or monsters, or large dogs, or burglars—that his fears limit his enjoyment of life, he may have a phobia. Even true phobias do not necessarily require outside treatment (especially in very young children). But they do require more patience and attention than everyday fears.

Negative Self-Image

A sensitive child might be shy, picky, fussy, or stubborn. But he should—ideally—like himself enough as he is. If he dwells relentlessly on his inadequacies, if he is constantly putting himself down, he may need some outside support.

Of course, many adolescents go through a breast-beating stage that isn't necessarily out of the ordinary. Normal teens (whether sensitive or not) balance those moods with periods of confidence and good spirits.

Allergies

If your child has low sensory threshold and has severe difficulty with certain foods, you may want to rule out food allergies before ascribing his sensitivity to temperament. Most "fussy" eaters who spit out new foods and demand that their food be prepared in certain ways are sensitive; some may have a genuine allergy.

Extreme Reactions

Are your sensitive child's reactions out of all proportion? If he has a trivial upsetting experience, does he cry for days? With normal children—even sensitive ones—even a powerful negative reaction eventually fades. If your child responds to difficulties in ways that seem seriously out of proportion, he may feel overwhelmed by his troubles and benefit from outside help.

Secondary Effects

Sometimes a sensitive child's troubles reach beyond temperament and generate effects in far-reaching areas of life—and affect others beyond himself.

Is your child's health being affected? Are his eating troubles harming his health, or are his nightmares keeping him from getting enough sleep?

Are his school anxieties affecting his school attendance, his placement or course selections, or his learning opportunities in school?

Is your child extremely fearful or afraid to leave home? Very anxious children suffer from more than just the fear. They also miss out on many opportunities for growth, and all the experiences that other children enjoy.

Are your sensitive child's troubles having a negative effect on other family members? If a child needs so much attention and help that another child is neglected, for example, the family may need outside help and support.

There's a difference between these behaviors and others that parents worry are limiting or will affect their child's future. If a parent says, "My son won't try out for the team, thus he is losing opportunities for athletic achievement and thus success and status in life," the chances are that the parent needs to put things in perspective.

Thoughts of Suicide

Is your sensitive child talking about suicide? Many children who are not deeply troubled do sometimes say, "I'll kill myself" when frustrated or angry. Parents should discuss their child's concerns and worries. But frequent talk of suicide signals the need for professional help.

If you feel that your sensitive child is struggling desperately, and you don't feel competent to help, do seek support. You might start with your pediatrician, who can recommend a therapist who works with families and children. Try to find a therapist who understands and honors temperament, and is willing to work within the context of your child's sensitivity.

SENSITIVE OUTCOMES

As adults, sensitive people make their own choices about how to manage and cope with their sensitivity. Some mask it, some work around it, some sit back and enjoy it.

"Because I'm so comfortable with solitary activities, I have to make an effort to stay in touch with people," said one socially sensitive adult. "I really do like being with people, but in limited doses. Sometimes I get so involved with my own pursuits that I drift toward isolation. When this happens, I have to make an effort to call old friends and re-connect. I know myself pretty well, and I know how to guard against going to extremes of isolation."

"I started my own business and deal with others all the time," said a formerly shy adult. "There's no way I could do the things I want to do and let shyness slow me down. I'm not really comfortable with some of these interactions, but I've taught myself how to cope and move on toward what I want to do."

"I remember hating camping, but now I'm glad they made me. I have wonderful memories of the way the forest smelled, of waking up at midnight when we camped on cots outside, and being dazzled by the brilliance of the stars. If my parents had given up and let me stay home, I would never have those memories."

"I'm an artist, and I enjoy the company of other people who also appreciate beauty. I don't feel I've had to make a lot of compromises or had to change my sensitivity. I've found my niche—and it happens to be a very fine niche!"

The persistent child who has trouble with change may become a focused, committed scholar, scientist, or community leader.

The shy child may become a thoughtful observer. The child who keeps his thoughts to himself becomes an analytical adult who prefers to think things through before speaking. He may be appreciated as a good, thoughtful listener.

As adults, sensitive people might be described as:

- Creative
- Empathic and intuitive
- Discriminating
- Focused and dedicated
- Artistic
- Thoughtful
- Independent
- Kind

Throughout history, people who were sensitive as children became distinguished in a range of fields.

Isaac Newton was bright, solitary, and preferred to play alone.

Albert Einstein was slow to talk, wouldn't play with other children, and did not adjust to school.

Gandhi was small, frail, and extremely shy.

Eleanor Roosevelt was painfully shy and had to train herself to socialize and to give speeches.

Marie Curie was serious, shy, and studious as a child.

Florence Nightingale was shy and timid as a child.

According to the historical psychologists Mildred and Victor Goertzel, eminent literary personalities as children "reacted sensitively to sounds, smells, colors, tastes, and the feel of things." In addition, they were intensely responsive to the emotional climate in their homes.

Historically, sensitive children may have been more likely to choose or be directed into solitary or creative occupations, like philosophy and the arts, rather than social and power-based occupations like politics and business.

But child-rearing techniques have evolved considerably in recent years, so it's difficult to tell if today's shy child is going to feel limited to traditional realms. Who's to say that a sensitive, thoughtful, intuitive, empathetic person couldn't develop into a leader? Such a person could provide much needed attributes to the world.

CONCLUSION

As Jerome Kagan stresses, sensitivity is not a weakness. A sensitive, highly reactive nervous system is not weaker or less robust than one that is slower to react. So the sensitive child is not necessarily at risk of emotional illness or any other difficulties.

In some ways, people with a tendency toward inhibition are actually protected from certain kinds of disastrous outcomes. Traits like aggression and impulsivity put people at higher risk for dangerous or criminal behavior.

As one teacher who has seen hundreds of children pass through her doors puts it, "We need all kinds of people. We need shy people, we need loud people, we need boisterous people. If they're shy, I want to modify their shyness. But I don't try to change their personality. My job is to respect who they are."

Sensitivity is a gift—a gift that does not come free. Sensitive people are more open to suffering than others, and they are open not only to their own suffering, but to that of others. The weight of the world and its injustices can weigh heavily on the shoulders of the sensitive.

But ultimately, the sensitive child has the gift of being open to the world and its delights in a way that less sensitive people are not. Your challenge is to bring up your sensitive child in such a way that he doesn't lose this gift but emerges from childhood still in possession of his unique birthright.

◈ 10 ◈

Questions and Answers

Q: *I have trouble establishing consistent discipline with my two daughters, who are seven and nine. My older girl gets deeply hurt whenever I discipline or criticize her. She really does not need much punishment, since she's well-behaved. But my younger daughter complains that whenever she misbehaves, I'm strict and take away privileges. I really can't use the same techniques with both children. How do I set limits for both girls that are fair and consistent, yet take into account what my sensitive child needs?*

A: Siblings are incredibly adept at picking up the slightest difference in the way they're treated. The chances are that even if your daughters had the same temperament, and you used the same discipline techniques with both, one or both would claim injustice.

Your best bet is to convey to your children that they are individuals and respond to limits and punishments differently. You can discuss temperament with both your daughters, so that each understands her own strengths and limitations, as well as the strengths and limitations of her sister.

However, in matters of discipline, it's important to look beyond temperament and concentrate on behavior. If your sensitive child really does get into trouble less frequently, then you are on solid ground if you explain that she doesn't get punished much for that reason.

Take care that your explanation doesn't come out like, "Why can't you be more like your sister?" Rather, you might say, "Melissa hasn't had time-out for a long time because she's been remembering the rules. We give reminders, and if the reminders work, then that's enough. If either one of you chooses to disobey the rules, then there's a consequence."

If you aren't being too solicitous with your sensitive child, and letting her get away with more mischief than her sister, your younger child should come to accept this.

Q: *My daughter is shy and frightened of strangers. Now that she's seven and able to go around the neighborhood on her own, I know I need to emphasize the importance of avoiding people she doesn't know. I know she is unlikely to approach or talk to a stranger, but how do I teach her the basic safety rules without terrifying her even more?*

A: We certainly do send conflicting signals to children. On one hand, we encourage them to say "Hello" when they meet people for the first time, and then we tell them that under no circumstances should they respond to an unknown adult who approaches them.

Certainly you need to remind your daughter that people are generally good, that the people you introduce her to are friendly and well-meaning.

Emphasize that these rules are like wearing a seat belt in the car. True, there are a tiny number of dangerous people, just as sometimes there are car accidents. We don't expect to ever have a car wreck, but we wear our belts all the time as an important safety habit.

If you emphasize the common sense safety rule aspect of this issue and avoid the idea that strangers are lying in wait for unsuspecting children, you should be able to put her fears into perspective.

You can also praise your child for her ability to be careful when she's away from you. You can say, "I always know that when you walk to Megan's house, that you'll be careful and sensible about safety. It makes me feel proud to know you can take good care of yourself."

Then you do need to go over the basic rules— no conversations with unfamiliar people she meets on the street, no getting in cars, no accepting of gifts—and to always run away from, and report, anyone who tries to approach her.

Q: *My five-year-old daughter is absolutely terrified of spiders. If she sees one, she cries and runs to us, demanding that we kill it. If she sees a picture of a spider in a book, she gets just as scared. Now she's saying that* *she doesn't want to go to our cabin in the mountains this summer because "it's full of spiders." What can we do to help her?*

A: Phobias about animals and insects are common among young children. Usually, you can help your child get past this discomfort by desensitization. She may never *like* spiders, but at least she can get to a point where spiders don't seem to dominate her life the way they do now.

First, check your own attitudes. Do *you* shudder and shake every time you encounter something with more than four legs? If so, you'll have a hard time persuading your daughter that spiders are okay. You'd better try to enlist another family member to work with your child on this issue (or get over your own discomfort).

The next step is to discuss this fear with your daughter and tell her that you're going to help her manage it. Then initiate a public relations program that puts spiders in a good light.

Look for picture books or nature books that show spiders in a harmless way. See if your daughter will look at friendly drawings of spiders, or listen to the story of *Charlotte's Web*. Talk about how spiders spin beautiful webs and are usually harmless to people. The more you stress the interesting facts about spiders, the more she will see them as something to learn about, rather than be frightened of.

Remind her how much bigger than the spider she is, and how she can always get away from one if she doesn't want to be near it.

When she's ready, you could show her photographs of different kinds of spiders in books and plan a trip to a nature museum to see real ones. If she reaches this stage, she'll certainly be ready for a visit to the cabin.

Q: *At meals, my seven-year-old son eats one food at a time. He'll eat all his potatoes, then all his vegetables, then all his meat. This seems odd to me. My husband does the same thing. Does this behavior have to do with adaptability? Sensitivity to change?*

A: Quite possibly. Children who are sensitive to change have a hard time switching gears and have an especially difficult time tearing themselves away from something they enjoy. If your son is enjoying his mashed potatoes, he wants to continue to enjoy them, rather than switch to chicken. Just be glad that he actually does get around to his vegetables!

Q: *When my daughter was three, my husband and I went on a trip and left her with a sitter for a week. When we got back, she was more clingy than usual, and ever since, she's been anxious when we leave and shy around strangers. Did our going away traumatize her? Is her anxiety something that can be changed?*

A: The idea that if certain distressing events take place at vulnerable times in a child's life, she will be permanently damaged is being reevaluated these days. Certainly distressing events have consequences for children's happiness and security. But in homes that are otherwise stable and loving, an isolated incident is not likely to leave lasting scars.

Many children whose parents have never taken any trips at all have children who are emotionally sensitive. Your daughter's anxieties may have been increased by your trip, but they should ease over time.

Q: *I understand that temperament may have a genetic component. Does this mean that certain temperaments run in families? It seems that most families I know have children with quite different personalities.*

A: People in families are not identical. No two have the same set of genes, unless they are identical twins. The number of possible combinations of traits that two parents could generate is limited only by the number of children they have. Even closely related people have different hair color, eye color, nose shape, and height, just as they have different interests, talents, and temperaments.

Q: *My son is adopted. His temperament is very different from mine. Will we have a harder time establishing a good fit?*

A: There will be many traits that differ between you and your son, including appearance and medical history. And certainly the aspects of his temperament that are genetic will come from his biological parents.

However, many children differ dramatically in temperament from their biological parents, as you can observe all around you. And children differ dramatically from their biological siblings, as well. In all families, parents delight in traits that surprise them. ("He's a great athlete! Where did *that* come from?")

You should be able to understand and celebrate your son's individuality and his temperament by using the same suggestions and techniques that apply to all families.

Q: *I have a hard time celebrating my eight-year-old daughter's temperament when she seems so inactive. She spends hours by herself, reading, writing stories, and playing with her cat. She is a slow starter in the morning, and even then she moves slowly.*

I'm just the opposite. I'm up and ready to roll at dawn, ready to get things done and enjoy life. It makes me extremely frustrated to watch her lethargy. I know I shouldn't condemn her, but it's hard for me to find that aspect of her behavior appealing. And then I feel bad because I don't like everything about my daughter. How can I view her temperament more positively?

A: Before our children are born, we parents fantasize about an ideal child, a soul mate who will be perfect and delightful in every way. Then when reality hits, we realize we have a real individual on our hands, not an extension of our own imagination.

Sometimes it's difficult to give up our dream. You, as an active, outgoing person, probably had hopes of sharing your energy and interests with your daughter. You may have imagined both of you jumping out of bed, zooming out the door, and sharing all sorts of adventures. But instead, you have a daughter who isn't at all like this.

Difficult as it may be, it is necessary to grieve for the perfect child, then move on to enjoying the wonderful child you do have. Eventually, you will be able to compartmentalize the old yearnings, rather than have them intrude on the real relationship you can forge with your real daughter.

Assuming that she is happy and thriving with her own sensitivity, you have much to celebrate. Your daughter will never be you, nor should she be.

Q: *My daughter is in fourth grade and is having a hard time with her teacher. The teacher has a regimented classroom, with every activity following a tight schedule. The children have very little flexibility. I was glad, at first, that Molly was assigned to this teacher, because I thought she'd do well with the regularity and predictability of the setting.*

But now she's quite unhappy. She has a lot of trouble with transitions, and her classroom is an all-day series of transitions. Every time she gets immersed in a project, it's time to clean up and move on to something else. Molly's always last in line because it takes her so long to finish a project or put away her materials. Would she be better off with another teacher, or should I force her to stick it out for the year?

A: Children who are sensitive to change certainly do have trouble with the demands of the school day, and a teacher who doesn't soften the edges of all those transitional times can be a difficult match for these sensitive children.

However, in managing a sensitive child, you

need to strike a balance between forcing her to adjust to the environment, and making the environment easier for your child. Sooner or later, Molly is going to have to cope with transitions in school, the workplace, and other aspects of her life. It's possible that your best approach is to use this year as an opportunity for her to improve her adaptability and to learn some techniques for coping with change a bit better than she has.

Perhaps you can discuss Molly's specific problems with the teacher and offer some suggestions.

- Molly might benefit from an "early warning system." Perhaps the teacher could notify her a few minutes before the rest of the class that it's time to begin to clean up her art project.
- She might be given certain classroom jobs that would help her be part of the transitions, such as distributing materials or collecting test papers afterward.
- You or your spouse might volunteer to be an aide or room parent, or to help out at classroom parties. If you can observe the dynamics of the class firsthand, you'll be better able to offer suggestions either to the teacher or to Molly.

If you conclude that Molly is suffering in this particular classroom, you'll want to consider asking to have her transferred. Barring extreme circumstances, however, Molly will do better if she uses this year as an opportunity to practice enlarging her skills and comfort level with transitions.

Q: *My ten-year-old son washes his hands frequently. He'll wash up for lunch, then touch something (not necessarily something dirty), then rush back and wash his hands again. His hands are getting chapped from all of this. I tell him once is enough, but it doesn't seem to help.*

I did talk to him about germs and the reasons why we should wash hands before eating, but I didn't mean for him to get carried away. He is a worrier, and he asks a lot of questions about germs and disease. Does he need special help or will he get over this on his own?

A: Excess hand washing is a compulsive behavior that is fairly manageable but can become limiting in later life if not dealt with. For most children, it's a habit, rather than a real disorder, and can be handled fairly easily.

Your son may be partially educated about germs, but not entirely. For example, he may not understand that one washing is enough (after using the toilet, before a meal). Also, if—as it appears—he is interested in germs and medicine, you can channel this interest. Give him more information. He can learn about "good" germs, such as bacteria that nourish the soil and help digest food. And he can understand that most household germs don't do much harm. If a cookie falls on the kitchen floor, it probably can still be eaten without harm.

Demonstrate proper hand washing. For most purposes (other than performing surgery), a quick soaping, a quick rinse, and a drying on a towel are all that's necessary, not a lengthy scrubbing. Demonstrate and have him time you.

Then, try involving him in "dirty" jobs and activities, like painting and gardening. Cooking and baking can feel "dirty," with all that dough and assorted juices getting all over. Your son can enjoy these activities and learn that he can get messy, then wash his hands when he's finished, and that's enough.

If these suggestions don't work, he should be evaluated by a professional to distinguish ordinary squeamishness from obsessive-compulsive disorder, which can be treated.

Q: *Although my daughter has a few friends, she doesn't interact easily with other kids, and I can't imagine her coping with the real world as she grows older. How can I get her to be assertive, to protect herself, to develop "street smarts" if she doesn't have many ways to learn this naturally from a wide circle of friends?*

A: This is a legitimate concern about sensitive children, especially the ones who don't get a lot of rough-and-ready interacting with their peers. As much as we celebrate sensitivity, we also want our children to be tough enough to cope with a sometimes hostile world.

But no child, sensitive or not, really picks up these skills naturally. In your daughter's case, you may be that teacher. As you have taught her safety rules since she was a baby, continue to teach age-appropriate skills as she matures.

You can practice assertive behaviors with her

and role-play specific situations that might come up. Play "what-if?" games with her.

For example, if your daughter is in her teen years, you could say, "You're walking down the street. Now I pull up next to you and say, 'Hey, let's go for a ride.' You don't know me, but I'm really cute. Now what?"

As your daughter grows older, you can encourage her to conduct more business or consumer transactions on her own, such as shopping, ordering food, making telephone calls to get information, and asking directions.

Q: *In trying to explain to my son's friends why his feelings were hurt, I know I shouldn't say, "He's sensitive" But I can't find another way to explain him.*

A: The term "sensitive" is useful for understanding your son's temperament as an immutable part of his makeup—he has a sensitive nervous system. However, that doesn't mean that the general public, including your son's friends, will respond to the term in a way that is helpful. They may hear, "thin-skinned" or "not macho" instead of the message you'd like to convey.

Therefore, it might be wiser to use terms that describe your son's preferences as they have appeared in the situation. "John may not have realized that you were just kidding," or, "He likes to take his time," or, "He'll respond better to a quiet voice."

Naturally, how you define your sensitive child to his peers depends considerably on his age. While your son is young, your explanations—and the terms you choose to use in your explanations—are important. But as he grows older, he needs to do more and more of the defining and interpreting himself.

Q: *My sensitive daughter is extremely jealous of her older sister, who is outgoing and popular. She compares herself to her sister and broods about her own inadequacies. How can I help my daughter in this situation?*

A: Sibling rivalry has always been with us, and it's just as much a problem in families where sensitivity is not an issue. However, when one child is sensitive and the other is decidedly not, the sensitive child is at risk of setting herself up for certain failure.

It's essential that you discuss temperament within your family and underscore that the differences in your family have to do with comfort, rather than merit. Your older daughter is outgoing and socially active because she enjoys doing that, not just because she is "better." That behavior does not come naturally to your younger child, and that does not mean that she is "worse."

Encourage your older daughter to be charitable when comparing herself with her sister, rather than crowing about all her accomplishments.

And try to encourage your sensitive child to define what she really wants for herself, independent of her sister. Does she really want to be "the most popular kid in school," or would she be happier with a few more friends and a bit more recognition? When she has clarified her goals, you and she can work toward reaching them.

Q: *Why does my son enjoy being alone so much? I would understand if he really wasn't at all social, but he is. He's eleven and has several close friends and a lot of acquaintances. But often on weekends, he won't go out and he won't call anyone to come over. Then the following weekend, he'll be very busy and see all his buddies. When he's alone, I worry that he's had a fight with his friends, or that he'll lose touch with them. What's going on?*

A: Your son seems like the kind of socially sensitive child who genuinely enjoys solitude—at least some of the time. Unlike truly shy people, socially sensitive people are not uncomfortable around others, as long as their social interactions are in manageable doses.

For a very social person, relating to others is pleasurable and energizing. The more people at the party, the happier they are. The longer the visitor stays, the better. For these people, there's a genuine letdown when the guests leave and they are all alone.

For the person with a tendency to be solitary, however, relating to other people takes effort and energy, so they need to rest from it periodically. This need to rest does not mean they dislike the interaction. To the contrary, they may find it quite enjoyable, just as you might enjoy playing tennis but feel the need to sit down and get your strength back after a few sets.

It seems that this describes your son quite well. He is happy, well-adjusted, and likes being with his friends. Then he likes to be alone for a period, to recharge his batteries. Later on, refreshed, he looks forward to being with people again, and ventures out into his social world.

As he grows older, he may need to cultivate diplomatic skills, so that he doesn't inadvertantly insult people when he retreats into solitude or doesn't reach out to them. It sounds, however, as though your son is managing his social sensitivity remarkably well.

Understanding what's happening emotionally and physically as your little one evolves from a baby into a child is a vital part of being an effective parent. In these helpful, down-to-earth guides, you'll learn what to expect and what to do at every stage of development. Filled with caring advice, *The Magical Years* helps you keep up with all of the many changes you'll encounter during this special time in your child's life.

THE MAGICAL YEARS

Janet Poland

GETTING TO KNOW YOUR ONE-YEAR-OLD
_____ 95418-2 $4.99 U.S./$5.99 Can.

SURVIVING YOUR TWO-YEAR-OLD
_____ 95582-0 $4.99 U.S./$5.99 Can.

MAKING FRIENDS WITH YOUR THREE-YEAR-OLD
_____ 95627-4 $4.99 U.S./$5.99 Can.

Publishers Book and Audio Mailing Service
P.O. Box 070059, Staten Island, NY 10307
Please send me the book(s) I have checked above. I am enclosing $_____ (please add $1.50 for the first book, and $.50 for each additional book to cover postage and handling. Send check or money order only—no CODs) or charge my VISA, MASTERCARD, DISCOVER or AMERICAN EXPRESS card.

Card Number_____

Expiration date_____Signature_____

Name_____

Address_____

City_____State/Zip _____
Please allow six weeks for delivery. Prices subject to change without notice. Payment in U.S. funds only. New York residents add applicable sales tax.   MY 8/95

CHILD CARE BOOKS YOU CAN COUNT ON—

from ST. MARTIN'S PAPERBACKS

BEYOND JENNIFER AND JASON
Linda Rosenkrantz and Pamela Redmond Satran
Newly updated, this landmark book is truly the only guide
you'll need to naming your baby!
_____ 95444-1 $4.99 U.S./$5.99 Can.

GOOD BEHAVIOR
**Stephen W. Garber, Ph.D., Marianne Daniels Garber, and
Robyn Freedman Spizman**
This comprehensive, bestselling guide lists answers to over
a thousand of the most challenging childhood problems.
_____ 95263-5 $6.99 U.S./$7.99 Can.

THE SELF-CALMED BABY
William A.H. Sammons, M.D.
Strung-out babies *can* calm themselves—and this one-of-
a-kind guide shows you how to help them do it!
_____ 92468-2 $4.99 U.S./$5.99 Can.

Publishers Book and Audio Mailing Service
P.O. Box 070059. Staten Island. NY 10307
Please send me the book(s) I have checked above. I am enclosing $ _____ (please add
$1.50 for the first book. and $.50 for each additional book to cover postage and handling.
Send check or money order only—no CODs) or charge my VISA. MASTERCARD
DISCOVER or AMERICAN EXPRESS card.

Card Number_____

Expiration date_____ Signature_____

Name_____

Address_____

City_____ State/Zip _____
Please allow six weeks for delivery. Prices subject to change without notice. Payment in
U.S. funds only. New York residents add applicable sales tax.
CCB 3/96

JANET POLAND is a writer, poet, and former newspaper editor who has written extensively about families and children for newspapers and magazines.

She graduated from Grinnell College and earned a graduate degree in political science from the University of Wisconsin. She worked in state government and in public television for several years before beginning a career in journalism. For more than a decade, she was a reporter, columnist, and editor on the staff of several daily newspapers in Pennsylvania, and received numerous journalism awards. More recently, as a free-lance journalist, her work has appeared frequently in the *Philadelphia Inquirer*.

She lives in Bucks County, Pennsylvania, with her husband and two sons.

JUDI CRAIG, PH.D., has counseled thousands of parents and children in more than twenty-seven years as a clinical psychologist. Readers are delighted with the common-sense approach of her most recent books, *Little Kids, Big Questions* and *Parents on the Spot*. Her "Parent Skills" column was featured for eight years in the *Sunday San Antonio Light*; her new column "Family Matters" appears in *Images*, a Sunday magazine in the *San Antonio Express News*. She has also consulted to corporations, agencies, schools, and psychiatric hospitals, and recently completed her training as a Master Practitioner in Neurolinguistic Programming. She is a frequent guest on national radio and television. She is the mother of three grown children, and lives in San Antonio, Texas.